BRAZIL, RUSSIA, INDIA, CHINA, AND SOUTH AFRICA

INVESTMENT CLIMATES

GLOBAL ECONOMIC STUDIES

Additional books in this series can be found on Nova's website
under the Series tab.

Additional E-books in this series can be found on Nova's website
under the E-book tab.

GLOBAL ECONOMIC STUDIES

BRAZIL, RUSSIA, INDIA, CHINA, AND SOUTH AFRICA

INVESTMENT CLIMATES

SANDRA C. OWENS
EDITOR

New York

Copyright © 2013 by Nova Science Publishers, Inc.

For permission to use material from this book please contact us:
Telephone 631-231-7269; Fax 631-231-8175
Web Site: http://www.novapublishers.com

Additional color graphics may be available in the e-book version of this book.

Library of Congress Cataloging-in-Publication Data

ISBN: 978-1-62618-627-9

Published by Nova Science Publishers, Inc. † New York

CONTENTS

PREFACE

An important component of economic statecraft, investment climate statements provide U.S. firms with country-specific information and assessments prepared by posts abroad on investment laws, measures, and other factors that may be useful in making business decisions. The Investment Climate Statements help identify the barriers and market distortions that too often deter U.S. investment, provide U.S. investors with the information they need to better assess business risks, and serve as a basis for engaging foreign governments on modernizing investment regimes.

In: Brazil, Russia, India, China, and South Africa   ISBN: 978-1-62618-627-9
Editor: Sandra C. Owens   © 2013 Nova Science Publishers, Inc.

Chapter 1

2013 INVESTMENT CLIMATE STATEMENT: BRAZIL*

Bureau of Economic and Business Affairs

OPENNESS TO, AND RESTRICTIONS UPON, FOREIGN INVESTMENT

Brazil is open to and encourages foreign direct investment. New foreign direct investment (FDI) into Brazil reached approximately USD 65 billion in 2012 and, according to the United Nations Conference on Trade and Development (UNCTAD) World Investment Report, Brazil is the fifth-most attractive country for FDI for the period of 2012-2014 and is consistently the largest FDI recipient in Latin America, typically receiving close to half of all South America's incoming FDI. The United States is a major foreign investor in Brazil; according to the Central Bank of Brazil, the United States had the highest stock of FDI in Brazil as of 2010, with US$104 billion. While Brazil is generally considered a friendly environment for foreign investment, complex tax and regulatory requirements exist. In most cases, these impediments apply without discrimination to both foreign and domestic firms. The Government of Brazil (GOB) generally makes no distinction between foreign and national capital in cases of direct investment.

---

* This is an edited, reformatted and augmented version of the Bureau of Economic and Business Affairs publication, dated February 2013.

The economy grew by around one percent in 2012, and independent analysts anticipate that it will rebound in 2013 and grow by around 3.2 percent. Medium- and long-term prospects remain favorable, supported by strong domestic demand, global demand for commodity exports, a growing middle class, expected investment in infrastructure and development of offshore oil reserves, and prudent macroeconomic policies.

Ownership Restrictions

FDI is prevalent across Brazil's economy, although certain sectors are subject to foreign ownership limitations. A 1995 constitutional amendment terminated the distinction between foreign and local capital in general, but there are laws that restrict foreign ownership within some sectors, notably aviation, insurance, and media.

Aviation
The Government of Brazil currently restricts foreign investment in domestic airline companies to a maximum of 20 percent. A bill pending in the Chamber of Deputies (PL6716) would increase that ceiling to 49 percent.

On March 19, 2011, representatives from the U.S. and Brazilian governments signed an Air Transport Agreement that will lead to an Open Skies relationship between the United States and Brazil, eliminating numerical limits on passenger and cargo flights between the two countries. If it is approved by Brazil's Congress, the agreement will take effect in October 2015. Both parties also signed a Memorandum of Consultation (MOC) that incrementally increases flight limits in the meantime. For example, in October 2012, the maximum number of weekly passenger flights was increased by 28 for U.S. airlines and by 28 for Brazilian airlines, and the maximum number of cargo flights allowed rose by 14 for each country's airlines. Additional increases will take effect in October 2013 and 2014.

Insurance
U.S. companies wanting to enter Brazil's insurance and reinsurance market must establish a subsidiary, enter into a joint venture, or acquire or partner with a local company. Market entry for banks may occur on a case-by-case basis. The Brazilian reinsurance market was opened to competition in 2007. In December 2010 and March 2011, however, the Brazilian National Council on Private Insurance (CNSP) effectively rolled back market

liberalization through the issuance of Resolutions 225 and 232, which disproportionately affect foreign insurers operating in the Brazilian market. Resolution 225 requires that 40 percent of all reinsurance risk be placed with Brazilian companies. Resolution 232 allows insurance companies to place only 20 percent of risk with affiliated reinsurance companies. In December 2011, the CNSP issued Resolution 241, which walked back some of the restrictions of Resolution 225 by allowing the 40 percent requirement to be waived if local reinsurance capacity does not exist.

Media

Open broadcast (non-cable) television companies are subject to a regulation requiring that 80 percent of their programming content be domestic in origin. Foreign cable and satellite television programmers are subject to an 11 percent remittance tax; however, the tax can be avoided if the programmer invests 3 percent of its remittances in co-production of Brazilian audio-visual services. In September 2011, President Rousseff signed into force a law covering the subscription television market, including satellite and cable TV that will remove the previous 49 percent limit on foreign ownership of cable TV companies. Under the law, telecom companies will be allowed to offer television packages with their service. Content quotas will require every channel to air at least three and a half hours per week of Brazilian programming during primetime. Additionally, one-third of all channels included in any TV package will have to be Brazilian. In order to gauge public opinion regarding the telecom sector before proposing revisions to existing regulations, the Brazilian Telecommunications Agency (ANATEL) organized three public consultations in late 2011 and submitted the results to the Brazilian Congress. As a result of feedback from the Brazilian Congress, the Brazilian Supreme Court will hold further consultations in February 2013. It is anticipated that revisions to regulations could be enacted in 2013. While the results of these consultations are being considered, the previously existing law still prevails.

Foreign investment restrictions remain in a limited number of other sectors, including highway freight (20 percent) and mining of radioactive ore. Foreign ownership of land within 150 km of national borders remains prohibited unless approved by Brazil's National Security Council. In October 2009, the Chamber of Deputies approved legislation that would further restrict foreign ownership of land along Brazil's borders and within the Amazon. The proposed legislation still requires passage by the Brazilian Senate, followed by presidential approval before it can become law.

On December 9, 2011, the National Land Reform and Settlement Institute (INCRA) published a set of new rules covering the purchase of Brazilian land by foreigners.

These rules follow an August 2010 Attorney General's opinion that similarly limited foreign agricultural land ownership. Under the new rules, the area bought or leased by foreigners cannot account for more than 25 percent of the overall area in any municipal district. Additionally, no more than 10 percent of the land in any given municipal district may be owned or leased by foreign nationals from the same country. The rules also make it necessary to obtain congressional approval before large plots of land can be purchased by foreigners, foreign companies, or Brazilian companies with the majority of shareholders from foreign countries. There are several proposed bills pending in the Brazilian Congress which would clarify the process for foreigners who want to purchase land.

Infrastructure Concession

Brazil has begun an ambitious program to draw in private capital and managerial expertise to upgrade the nation's infrastructure. In February 2012, Brazil auctioned off concessions for the right to operate three of its largest airports – Juscelino Kubitschek (Brasilia), Guarulhos (Sao Paulo), and Viracopos (Campinas) – to the private sector. In December 2012, President Rousseff announced plans to auction in September 2013 additional concessions to operate the airports of Galeão (Rio de Janeiro) and Confins (Belo Horizonte).

In August 2012, government authorities announced plans to auction concessions for the right to build and operate over 6,200 miles of railroad as well as 3,500 miles of highway. Between those two projects, the Brazilian Government hopes to attract US$ 66.5 billion in private investment in roads and railroad in the next 20 years, with US$ 39.7 billion of that figure coming in the next five years.

Finally, in December 2012, President Rousseff announced plans to attract US$ 26 billion in private investment into the country's port sector within four years.

All of the infrastructure concessions are open to foreign companies. In fact, in the airport concessions, foreign companies have not only been encouraged to bid, but the auction criteria have been defined in a way that has the effect of requiring the participation of foreign airport operators. The bidding process is non-discriminatory, transparent, and performed without political interference.

Investment Goals

Between January 2011 and September 2012, the government's Program to Accelerate Growth (PAC) program disbursed US$191 billion, amounting to 40.4 percent of the spending total projected by the end of 2014. Under the program, an estimated R$959 billion was allocated for the period of 2011 through 2014. The government continues to indicate it is interested in attracting foreign investment to fund infrastructure projects.

In August 2011, Brazil announced a new industrial policy, *Plano Brasil Maior* (the "Bigger Brazil" plan), to support domestic producers, encourage investment, and spur innovation. The plan, covering the period of 2011-2014, sets targets for investment spending to reach 22.4 percent of GDP by 2014, up from a 2010 baseline of 18.4 percent. Private investment in R&D is to reach 0.90 percent of GDP by 2014, up from the 2010 figure of 0.59 percent. *Brasil Maior* also sets targets for making the economy more energy-efficient, reducing the amount of petroleum used per unit of GDP by 9 percent, and nearly tripling broadband internet penetration from 13.8 million households in 2010 to 40 million households in 2014.

The latest OECD Economic Survey for Brazil was released in 2011 and includes sections on regulatory environment, licensing, sectoral analysis, and impediments to investment. The Survey recommends continued fiscal consolidation, increased investment and savings, and additional infrastructure spending, all while incorporating the principles of social and environmental sustainability. The report can be found at: http://www.oecd.org/dataoecd/12/37/48930900.pdf.

Selected indicators from reputable third party sources

Measure	Year	Brazil Rank/Total
TI Corruption Perceptions	2012	69/176
Heritage Economic Freedom	2012	99/179
World Bank Ease of Doing Business	2013	130/185

Conversion and Transfer Policies

There are few restrictions on converting or transferring funds associated with a foreign investment in Brazil. Foreign investors may freely convert Brazilian currency in the unified foreign exchange market wherein buy-sell rates are determined by market forces. All foreign exchange transactions, including identifying data, must be reported to the Central Bank. Foreign exchange transactions on the current account have been fully liberalized.

Foreigners investing in Brazil must register their investment with the Central Bank within 30 days of the inflow of resources to Brazil. Registration is done electronically. Investments involving royalties and technology transfer must be registered with Brazil's patent office, the National Institute of Industrial Property (INPI). Investors must also have a local representative in Brazil. Portfolio investors must have a Brazilian financial administrator and register with the Brazilian Securities Exchange Commission (CVM).

All incoming foreign loans must be approved by the Central Bank. In most instances, the loans are automatically approved. Automatic approval is not issued when the costs of the loan are "not compatible with normal market conditions and practices." In such instances, the Central Bank may request additional information regarding the transaction. Foreign loans obtained abroad do not require advance approval by the Central Bank, provided the recipient is not a government entity. Loans to government entities, however, require prior approval from the Brazilian Senate as well as from the Finance Ministry Treasury Secretariat, and must be registered with the Central Bank.

Interest and amortization payments specified in a loan contract can be made without additional approval from the Central Bank. Early payments can also be made without additional approvals, if the contract includes a provision for them. Otherwise, early payment requires notification to the Central Bank to ensure accurate records of Brazil's stock of debt.

Foreign investors, upon registering their investment with the Central Bank, are able to remit dividends, capital (including capital gains), and, if applicable, royalties. Remittances must also be registered with the Central Bank. Dividends cannot exceed corporate profits. The remittance transaction may be carried out at any bank by documenting the source of the transaction (evidence of profit or sale of assets) and showing that applicable taxes have been paid.

Capital gain remittances are subject to a 15 percent income withholding tax, with the exception of the capital gains and interest payments on tax-exempt domestically issued Brazilian bonds. Repatriation of the initial investment is also exempt from income tax. Lease payments are assessed a 15 percent withholding tax.

Remittances related to technology transfers are not subject to the tax on credit, foreign exchange, and insurance, although they are subject to a 15 percent withholding tax and an extra 10 percent Contribution of Intervention in the Economic Domain (CIDE).

The Government of Brazil imposes the IOF, a tax on financial operations, on portfolio capital inflows. The main goal of the tax is to discourage short-term, speculative capital flows that could lead to excessive currency volatility or significant appreciation pressures on the Brazilian currency. The GOB made several tweaks to the IOF over the course of 2012 based on changes in the size and pace of portfolio inflows into Brazil and developments in international financial markets. The IOF ended the year at 6.0 percent of all foreign loans with terms of 720 days or less used to fund operations in Brazil. Those with a longer maturity are exempt. Profits and FDI remittances must pay an IOF of 0.38 percent.

Expropriation and Compensation

There have been no expropriation actions in Brazil against foreign interests in the recent past, nor have there been any signs that the current government is contemplating such actions. In the past, some claims regarding land expropriations by state agencies have been judged by courts in U.S. citizens' favor. However, compensation has not always been paid as states have filed appeals to these decisions, and the Brazilian judicial system moves slowly.

Dispute Settlement

The Brazilian court system, in general, is overburdened, and contract disputes can be lengthy and complex. The 2013 World Bank "Doing Business" survey found that on average it takes 44 procedures and 731 days to litigate a contract breach at an average cost of 16.5 percent of the claim.

Article 34 of Brazilian Law 9,307, the 1996 Brazilian Arbitration Act, defines a foreign arbitration judgment as any judgment rendered outside the national territory. The law established that the Brazilian Federal Supreme Court must ratify foreign arbitration awards. Law 9,307 also stipulates that the foreign arbitration award is to be recognized or executed in Brazil in conformity with the international agreements ratified by the country and, in their absence, with domestic law. (Note: A 2001 Federal Supreme Court ruling established that the 1996 Brazilian Arbitration Act, permitting international arbitration subject to Federal Supreme Court ratification of arbitration decisions, does not violate the Federal Constitution's provision that "the law shall not exclude any injury or threat to a right from the consideration of the Judicial Power.")

Brazil has ratified the 1975 Inter-American Convention on International Commercial Arbitration (Panama Convention), the 1979 Inter-American Convention on Extraterritorial Validity of Foreign Judgments and Arbitration Awards (Montevideo Convention) and the 1958 U.N. Convention on the Recognition and Enforcement of Foreign Arbitration Awards (New York Convention). Brazil, however, is not a member of the International Center for the Settlement of Investment Disputes (ICSID), also known as the Washington Convention.

Brazil has a commercial code that governs most aspects of commercial association, except for corporations formed for the provision of professional services, which are governed by the civil code. In 2005, bankruptcy legislation (Law 11101) went into effect creating a system, modeled on Chapter 11 of the U.S. bankruptcy code, which allows a company in financial trouble to negotiate a restructuring with its creditors outside of the courts. In the event a company does fail despite restructuring efforts, the reforms give creditors improved ability to recover their debts.

Brazil has both a federal and a state court system, and jurisprudence is based on civil law. Federal judges hear most disputes in which one of the parties is the State and rule on lawsuits between a foreign State or international organization and a municipality or a person residing in Brazil. Five regional federal courts hear appeals of federal judges' decisions.

Performance Requirements and Incentives

The Brazilian government uses a variety of tax incentives and attractive financing through the National Bank for Economic and Social Development (BNDES) to actively encourage both domestic and foreign investment. In 2012, BNDES disbursements rose 12 percent to reach R$156 billion, making it the largest development bank in the world, outpacing the lending of even the World Bank. BNDES funding in 2012 was focused on industry and infrastructure, with R$18.9 billion for the electricity sector, R$15.5 billion for transportation, and R$8.5 billion for chemicals and petrochemicals. BNDES also actively promotes development in traditionally underserved populations and regions of the country and in other potentially less profitable ventures, but the majority of lending takes place in the more industrialized regions of the country. A 2004 Public-Private Partnership (PPP) investment law promotes joint ventures in otherwise marginally profitable infrastructure investments.

The Government of Brazil extends tax benefits for investment in less developed parts of the country, for example the Northeast and the Amazon regions, with equal application to foreign and domestic investors. These incentives have been successful in attracting major foreign plants to areas like the Manaus Free Trade Zone, but most foreign investment remains concentrated in the more industrialized southern part of Brazil.

Individual states have sought to attract investment by offering ad hoc tax benefits and infrastructure support to specific companies, negotiated on a case by case basis. These benefits have spurred a so-called "fiscal war" between the states, with some states challenging the tax benefits as harmful fiscal competition. In June 2011, the Brazilian Supreme Court ruled that the benefits granted by 14 states on interstate commerce are unconstitutional, as they were implemented without unanimous consent from the National Council of Fiscal Policy (Confaz). In November 2012, the Ministry of Finance proposed to Congress an end to the "fiscal war" by setting the interstate tax rate on goods at 4 percent for all states, thus limiting states' ability to offer special tax incentives to attract investment away from other states. A decision on this proposal by Congress is expected in early 2013, but previous attempts at interstate tax reform have failed to gain Congressional support.

In October 2012, the GOB announced Decree 7819 in support of domestic auto manufacturers. The decree raised the Industrial Products Tax (IPI) by 30 percentage points of the price of the vehicle on all vehicle sales in the Brazilian market on or after January 1, 2013. This change affected all vehicles: domestically-produced, imports from other Mercosur member countries, imports from Mexico within quota, and all other foreign imports. Auto manufacturers are able to apply for a tax credit based on their ability to meet certain criteria, including the number of manufacturing processes performed in Brazil, enhancing fuel efficiency, committing to research and development investment in Brazil or Brazilian engineering services, and agreeing to participate in a fuel-efficiency labeling scheme. This decree is the successor to the September 2011 decree (No. 7567) which called for a 30 percentage point increase in the IPI on any car not sourced with at least 65 percent of parts from Merciful countries or Mexico, with which Brazil has an auto sector trade agreement. Decree 7567 expired on December 31, 2012. Both decrees are clear moves to encourage manufacturers to produce in Brazil rather than exporting cars to Brazil.

In December 2011, the Government of Brazil passed Law 12546, which introduced the Special Regime for the Reinstatement of Taxes for Exporters, dubbed the Reintegra Program. Exporters of products covering 8,630 tariff codes – representing R$80 billion of exports – will receive a subsidy of 3 percent of the value of their exports, to be used either as a credit against their income tax or as a cash payment. To qualify, the imported content of the exported goods must not exceed 40%, except in the case of high-tech goods, such as pharmaceuticals, electronics, and aircraft and parts, which are permitted to have up to 65% of inputs imported. In addition, Reintegra exempts exporters from so-called indirect taxes on capital expenditures, including the PIS/Cofins social contribution taxes and the IOF tax on financial transactions. The Reintegra Program, originally scheduled to expire at the end of 2012, was extended by the Ministry of Finance until December 31, 2013.

In December 2011, as part of the Plano Brasil Maior, the government of Brazil approved a corporate payroll tax exemption to businesses within the sectors of industry, trade and services. The measure originally ordered the exemption of payroll taxes for companies within the information technology, textile, leather and footwear sectors. At the end of 2012, the payroll exemption was extended to a total of 42 sectors to include construction metals, big appliances and pharmaceutical products for example. The measure replaced the 20 percent payroll tax for social security contributions with a rate between 1 and 2 percent of company gross operating revenue (less export revenue).

In May of 2010, the government placed state-owned communications firm Telebras at the head of a National Broadband Plan which incorporates fiscal incentives, private sector participation, and regulatory reform to build out Brazil's next generation communication infrastructure network. While the plan provides commercial opportunities for the private sector, including foreign investors, the government seeks to leverage the plan to advance Brazilian technology. This includes favorable BNDES financing for acquisition of telecom equipment that utilizes Brazilian technology, tax exemptions on the purchase of IT equipment that uses Brazilian technology, as well as favoring domestic technology in the procurement process.

As of October 2011, internet companies in Brazil began to offer broadband for as low as R$35.00 (US$19) per month. The "Internet for the People" initiative, part of the National Broadband Plan, aims to bring high-speed connections to 40 million homes, part of the government's efforts to increase digital inclusion throughout Brazilian society. The GOB seeks to connect all Brazilian municipalities to the internet no later than 2014. In addition to cutting the price of internet connections in half, the Brazilian government will provide free internet access to 59,000 public elementary and high schools. In the most marginal communities including rural settlements and indigenous communities, the Ministry of Communication will establish 13,000 Telecenters to boost digital inclusion.

To promote Brazilian industry, the Special Agency for Industrial Financing (FINAME) of BNDES provides financing for Brazilian firms to purchase Brazilian-made machinery and equipment and capital goods with a high level of domestic content. The interest rates charged by BNDES are often significantly lower than the prevailing market interest rates for domestic financing.

Government Procurement

Brazil is not a signatory to the WTO Agreement on Government Procurement (GPA). U.S. companies seeking to participate in Brazil's public sector procurement effectively need to partner with a local firm or have operations in Brazil. Foreign companies are often successful in obtaining subcontracting opportunities with large Brazilian firms that win government contracts.

Law 8666 (1993) covers most government procurement other than information technology/telecommunications and requires non-discriminatory treatment for all bidders regardless of nationality or origin of the product or service. Brazilian government procurement rules apply to purchases by government entities and state-owned companies. Brazil has an open competition process for major government procurements. The Brazilian government may not make a distinction between domestic and foreign-owned companies during the tendering process; however, when two equally qualified vendors are considered, the law's implementing regulations provide for a preference to Brazilian goods and services. Price is to be the overriding factor in selecting suppliers (see update in the following paragraph). However, the law's implementing regulations also allow for the consideration of non-price factors, giving preferences to certain goods produced in Brazil and stipulating local content requirements for fiscal benefits eligibility. Additionally, nearly all bids require establishment of a local representative for any foreign company bidding.

Brazil continued to apply preference margins to government procurement in 2012. In 2010, then-President Lula signed a decree that later was approved by the Congress and became law (No. 12,349, December 15, 2010), giving preference to firms that produce in Brazil -- whether foreign-owned or Brazilian -- that fulfill certain economic stimulus requirements such as generating employment or contributing to technological development, even when their bids are up to 25 percent more expensive than competing imported products. In August 2011, this system of preference margins was folded into Plano Brasil Maior. Government procurement is just one of thirty-five components under Brasil Maior intended to support Brazilian industry and protect domestic producers, particularly the labor-intensive sectors threatened by imports. The textile, clothing and footwear industries – among the few industries to have lost jobs during the current growth period – were the first to benefit from Brasil Maior when, in November 2011, the Ministry of Development, Industry and Commerce implemented an 8 percent preference margin for domestic producers in these industries when bidding on government contracts. In April 2012, Decrees 7709 and 7713 expanded the use of preference margins to pharmaceuticals and medicine (8 or 20 percent) and excavators and bulldozers (15 and 25 percent).

Decree 7174 (2010), which regulates the procurement of information technology goods and services, requires federal agencies and parastatal entities to give preferential treatment to domestically produced computer products and goods or services with technology developed in Brazil based on a complicated price/technology matrix.

Right to Private Ownership and Establishment

Foreign and domestic private entities may establish, own, and dispose of business enterprises.

Protection of Property Rights

Mortgages

Brazil has a system in place for mortgage registration, but implementation is uneven and there is no standardized contract. Foreign individuals or foreign-owned companies can purchase real property in Brazil. These buyers frequently arrange alternative financing in their own countries, where rates may be more attractive. Law 9514 (1997) helped spur the mortgage industry by establishing a legal framework for a secondary market in mortgages and streamlining the foreclosure process, but the mortgage market in Brazil is still underdeveloped, and foreigners may have difficulty obtaining mortgage financing. Large U.S. real estate firms, nonetheless, are expanding their portfolios in Brazil.

Intellectual Property Rights

Brazil is a signatory to the GATT Uruguay Round Agreements, including the Trade Related Aspects of Intellectual Property (TRIPs) Agreement, which it signed in 1994. Brazil is a signatory of the Bern Convention on Artistic Property, the Patent Cooperation Treaty, the Convention on Plant Variety Protection, and the Paris Convention on Protection of Intellectual Property.

Brazil is not a party to the WIPO Copyright Treaty or the WIPO Performances and Phonograms Treaty (collectively, the "WIPO Internet Treaties"). In 2006, Brazil announced plans to join the Madrid Agreement Concerning the International Registration of Marks ("Madrid Protocol"), but the executive branch has yet to submit this proposal to the Brazilian Congress for approval.

In most respects, Brazil's 1996 Industrial Property Law (Law 9279) meets the international standards specified in the TRIPs Agreement regarding patent and trademark protection. However, the law permits the grant of a compulsory license if a patent owner has failed to locally manufacture the patented invention in Brazil within three years of patent issuance, a form of compulsory licensing that the United States believes would be inconsistent with Articles 27.1 and 28.1 of TRIPs. On May 4, 2007, invoking TRIPS provisions for public health emergencies, Brazil issued a compulsory license for an anti-retroviral drug used in treating HIV/AIDS.

The United States continues to raise concerns regarding article 229-C of law 9279, as amended by Law 10196 (2001), which includes a requirement for the National Health Surveillance Agency (ANVISA) to grant an approval prior to the issuance of a pharmaceutical patent by the National Industrial Property Institute (INPI). Due to ANVISA's role in reviewing pharmaceutical patent applications – known as "prior consent" – there is a significant backlog in the issuance of patents. In addition, conflicting opinions on patentability between INPI and ANVISA have left more than 140 patent applications unissued. On October 16, 2009, the Brazilian Federal Attorney General (AGU), analyzing the institutional role of ANVISA in the patent application process, presented Opinion No. 210, which stated that ANVISA should examine pharmaceutical patent applications only from a public health perspective. The opinion states that INPI is the only agency with the competency to review the patentability requirements of such applications. On January 10, 2011, the AGU issued another opinion noting ANVISA's limited role, saying "ANVISA may not refuse the granting of the prior consent of art. 229-C of IP Law based on patentability requirements." The AGU´s opinions were not binding, and the Brazilian Federal Government created an Inter-Ministerial working group to study how to best implement the AGU's opinions.

On May 24, 2012, Inter-Ministerial Ruling no. 1056 was published, reporting the outcome of the working group. According to the ruling, all patent applications claiming pharmaceutical products and/or processes are to be initially analysed by ANVISA. If ANVISA grants its approval, then it will be assessed by the INPI. No other industrial sector is treated in this way. For all other patent applications, INPI is the sole arbiter of whether or not a patent is granted, and other agencies regulate market access.

On October 17, 2012, ANVISA opened public consultations on its proposed new regulations for prior consent. The new regulations reverse the existing workflow of pharmaceutical patent applications, as suggested by Ruling no. 1056. They also permit ANVISA´s analyses of patent applications to go beyond a public health perspective, to include patentability standards that are traditionally the domain of patent offices worldwide. The deadline to comment on the new regulations was December 20, 2012. It is unclear when the proposed regulations will be promulgated. The final result may have an effect on both product availability and capital inflows for the sector. If the system as currently proposed goes forward it may diminish the likelihood that newer "on patent" medications will be produced or even sold in Brazil.

An additional ongoing concern is the backlog of pending patent applications at INPI. INPI claims it takes an average of five years to receive a patent in Brazil; independent resources, however, state that it takes six to seven years. INPI has increased its hiring and training of new patent examiners in an effort to decrease pendency. In March 2013, INPI plans to begin rolling out an electronic filing system for new patent applications, which would enable inventors to file a patent application using an online system.

The United States has also raised concerns regarding Brazil's protection against unfair commercial use of test data generated in connection with obtaining marketing approval for human-use pharmaceutical products. Law 10603 (2002) covers data confidentiality for veterinary pharmaceuticals, fertilizers, agro-toxins, and related products, but does not cover pharmaceuticals for human use, which potentially inhibits the introduction of certain products into the market since a generic manufacturer can produce a copy locally and rely upon the safety and efficacy data of the originator.

A Brazilian government-drafted bill to provide protection for the layout design of integrated circuits (computer mask works) was enacted into law on May 31, 2007 (Law 11.484).

Patent and trademark licensing agreements must be recorded with and approved by INPI and registered with the Central Bank of Brazil (Normative Act No. 135, of April 15, 1997). Licensing contracts must contain detailed information about the terms of the agreement and royalties to be paid. In such arrangements, Brazilian law limits the amount of the royalty payment that can be taken as a tax deduction (from one percent to five percent), which consequently acts as a de facto cap on licensing fees (Act No. 436 of 1958).

Brazil's 1998 copyright law generally conforms to international standards, yet piracy of copyrighted material remains a problem. The Brazilian Congress passed a law in July 2003 increasing minimum prison sentences for copyright violations and establishing procedures for making arrests and the destruction of confiscated products. Draft Law 333 of 1999 would stiffen the criminal penalties for counterfeiting, but it remains stalled in the Brazilian Congress. After being shelved in 2006, the draft law was re-submitted in November 2008 for urgent reconsideration, but the proposal has still not come to a vote.

In August 2007, a bill (PL 1807/07) was introduced that, if approved, would amend Article 189 of Brazil's Industrial Property Law (Law 9279 of 1996) to increase the criminal penalties for trademark violations to two to six years, up from the current three to twelve months. The bill was approved by the House and sent to the Senate in June 2012, where it is currently being analyzed.

In the U.S. Trade Representative's 2007 Special 301 Report, Brazil was downgraded from "Priority Watch List" to "Watch List," in recognition of its improved anti-piracy enforcement efforts. Since then, Brazil has remained on the "Watch List" of the Special 301 Reports. Anti-piracy enforcement has continued to improve, especially in the major cities of Sao Paulo, Rio de Janeiro, and Brasilia. The upcoming 2014 FIFA soccer World Cup and 2016 Olympics will continue to drive this trend of strong anti-piracy and anti-counterfeiting efforts by local, state, and federal police.

Transparency of the Regulatory System

In the 2013 World Bank 'Doing Business' report, Brazil ranked 130th out of 185 countries in terms of overall ease of doing business, a decline of four places versus the 2012 report. According to the study, it takes an average of 13 procedures and 119 days to start a new business, significantly longer than the OECD high-income economies' average of 11.8 days. The study noted that the annual administrative burden to a medium-size business of tax payments in Brazil is an average of 2,600 hours versus 176 hours in the OECD high-income economies. According to this same study, the total tax rate for Brazil's medium-sized business is 69.3 percent of profits, compared to 42.7 percent in the OECD high-income economies. Business managers often complain of not understanding tax regulations, despite best efforts including large tax and accounting departments.

Tax regulations, while burdensome and numerous, do not differentiate between foreign and domestic firms. However, there have been instances of complaints that the value-added tax collected by individual states (ICMS) favors local companies. Although the tax is designed to be refunded upon export of goods outside of the country, exporters in many states have had difficulty receiving their ICMS rebates. Taxes on commercial and financial transactions are particularly burdensome, and businesses complain that these taxes hinder the international competitiveness of Brazilian-made products.

Of Brazil's ten federal regulatory agencies, the most prominent include ANVISA, the Brazilian FDA equivalent having regulatory authority over the production and marketing of food, drugs and medical devices; ANATEL, the country's telecommunication agency handling licensing and assigning bandwidth, ANP, the National Petroleum Agency regulating oil and gas contracts and overseeing the bidding process to acquire oil blocks, including for pre-salt oil; and ANAC, the agency overseeing the civil aviation industry. In addition to these federal regulatory agencies, Brazil has 23 state-level agencies and eight municipal-level agencies. Despite the existence of these bodies, the lack of a formal, federal-level institution tasked with coordinating the regulatory framework can often complicate Brazil's regulatory process.

The Office of the Presidency's Program for the Strengthening of Institutional Capacity for Management in Regulation (PRO-REG), created in 2007, has tried to introduce a broad program for improving the regulatory framework in Brazil, but lacks the authority to act as a single coordinating agency.

Pursuant to the Rousseff administration's priority to improve transparency, the general public has online access to both approved and proposed federal legislation, via websites for the Chamber of Deputies, Federal Senate, and the Office of the Presidency. While there is currently no system in place for public comment on these proposed laws and regulations, this has been identified by the Brazilian government as a key priority in improving Brazil's regulatory system.

Foreign investors have encountered obstacles when interfacing with regulatory agencies. Notable examples include companies in the electric power sector that have complained about the high level of regulatory risk, including the tariff review process. Additionally, some industries have reported challenges in obtaining licenses from IBAMA, the environmental regulator; citing unpredictability in IBAMA's licensing requirements, though the process has reportedly become more streamlined since 2008. There have also been examples of federal agencies levying significant fines on U.S. companies. In October 2011, Brazilian private insurance regulator (SUSEP) announced its intention to fine U.S. insurance company National Western Life US$ 6 billion for selling insurance contracts without being licensed in Brazil. The fine, which would be the largest in the history of Brazil's financial system, was upheld by SUSEP in mid-2012 and is currently under appeal. In 2012, various Brazilian regulatory agencies including IBAMA, Brazil's National Petroleum Agency (ANP), and the Rio de Janeiro State Institute of Environment (INEA) imposed separate fines on Chevron for damages related to a November 2011 offshore oil seep from near a Chevron-operated well; the ANP fines were eventually reduced to US$ 12 million and was paid by Chevron in September 2012. As of January, 2013, regulators had not yet granted Chevron approval to resume operations. Brazilian private sector organizations, which often include foreign companies, are vocal and involved in industry standards setting.

Regulatory review of mergers and acquisitions are carried out by the Administrative Council for Economic Defense (CADE). In October 2012, Brazil performed its first-ever pre-merger review of a pending merger, bringing Brazil in line with U.S. and European practices. Brazil had previously performed only post-merger reviews. This shift in merger review was a result of 2011 legislation (law 12,529) which was adopted to modernize Brazil's antitrust review and to combine the antitrust functions of the Ministry of Justice and the Ministry of Finance into those of the so-called Super CADE. This new government body will be responsible for enforcement of competition laws, consumer defense, and combating abuse of economic power.

Efficient Capital Markets and Portfolio Investment

The Brazilian financial sector is large and sophisticated. Banks lend at Brazilian market rates which, while they have fallen since 2011, remains high.

Reasons cited by industry observers include high taxation, repayment risk, concern over inconsistent judicial enforcement of contracts, high mandatory reserve requirements, and administrative overhead.

The financial sector is concentrated, with 2012 Central Bank data indicating that the 10 largest commercial banking institutions account for approximately 81 percent of financial sector assets, less brokerages (approx. US$ 2 trillion). Three of the five largest banks (in assets) in the country, Banco do Brasil, Caixa Economica Federal, and BNDES, are partially or completely federally owned. Lending by the large banking institutions is focused on the largest companies, while small and medium banks primarily serve small and medium-sized companies, but with a much smaller capital base.

The Central Bank has strengthened bank audits, implemented more stringent internal control requirements, and tightened capital adequacy rules to better reflect risk. It also established loan classification and provisioning requirements. These measures are applied to private and publicly owned banks alike. The Brazilian Securities and Exchange Commission (CVM) independently regulate the stock exchanges, brokers, distributors, pension funds, mutual funds, and leasing companies with penalties against insider trading.

Credit Market

Brazil's credit market has grown significantly over the past several years. Real interest rates, once among the highest in the world, fell dramatically in 2012, driven by continued decreases in the Central Bank's benchmark overnight Selic lending rate and a concerted effort by the GOB to reduce lending spreads charged by public and private banks. While local private sector banks are beginning to offer longer credit terms, BNDES, the government national development bank, is the traditional Brazilian source of longer-term credit, and also provides export credits. FINAME (the Special Agency for Industrial Financing) provides foreign and domestically owned companies operating in Brazil financing for the manufacturing and marketing of capital goods. FINAMEX (Export Financing), which finances capital good exports for both foreign and domestic companies, is a part of FINAME. One of the goals of these financing options is to support the purchase of domestically produced over imported equipment and machinery.

Equity Market

All stock trading is performed on the Sao Paulo Stock Exchange (BOVESPA), while trading of public securities is conducted on the Rio de

Janeiro market. In 2008, the Brazilian Mercantile & Futures Exchange (BM&F) merged with the BOVESPA to form what is now the fourth largest exchange in the Western Hemisphere, after the NYSE, NASDAQ, and Canadian TSX Group exchanges. BOVESPA has launched a "New Market," in which the listed companies comply with stricter corporate governance requirements. A majority of Initial Public Offerings are now listed on the New Market. In 2012, twelve new IPOs and follow-ons raised R$ 13 billion in capital; approximately 36 percent of this amount was foreign capital.

At the end of 2012, there were 452 companies traded on the BM&F/BOVESPA. Total daily trading average volume has risen from R$ 2.4 billion in 2006 to R$ 7.2 billion in 2012, and the number of trades has increased more than 10 times over the same period.

The BM&F/BOVESPA currently has no competition, but that may change soon. In January 2013, Direct Edge, the fourth-largest stock exchange operator in the United States, announced that it would shortly apply for a license to launch its services in Brazil in 2013. If the plan is approved by Brazil regulators, Direct Edge will serve as an alternative trading platform to the BOVESPA. Foreign investors, both institutions and individuals, can directly invest in equities, securities and derivatives. Foreign investors are required to trade derivatives and stocks of publicly held companies on established markets. At year-end 2012, foreign investors accounted for 40.3 percent of the total turnover on the BOVESPA. Domestic institutional investors were the second most active market participants, accounting for 32 percent of activity. Individual investors comprised 17.9 percent of activity, followed by financial institutions (8.1 percent), and public and private companies (1.9 percent). Law 10303 of 2001 limits preferred shares to 50 percent of new issuances.

Wholly owned subsidiaries of multinational accounting firms, including the major U.S. firms, are present in Brazil. As of 1996, auditors are personally liable for the accuracy of accounting statements prepared for banks.

In recent years the government has sought to manage short-term capital inflows and appreciation of the Brazilian currency with the introduction of new taxes on capital inflows (see "Conversion and Transfer Policies" section above).

Competition from State-Owned Enterprises

In the 1990's and early 2000s, the Brazilian government privatized state enterprises across a broad spectrum of industries, including mining, steel, aeronautics, banking, energy, and electricity generation and distribution. While the government has divested itself from many of its state-owned companies, it maintains partial control (at both the federal and state level) of some previously wholly state-owned enterprises. Notable examples of partially federally-controlled firms include energy giant Petrobras and power utility Eletrobras. Both Petrobras and Eletrobras include non-government shareholders, are listed on both the Brazilian and NYSE stock exchanges, and are subject to the same accounting and audit regulations as all publicly traded Brazilian companies.

The 2010 pre-salt legislation gives Petrobras sole operator status for the development of the new oil discoveries. The terms and conditions of the new regime favor Petrobras as the sole operator, although foreign firms are still anticipated to play a role in the pre-salt oil fields.

In addition to major players like Petrobras and Eletrobras, the Brazilian government, at both the federal and state levels, maintains ownership interests in a variety of other smaller enterprises. Typically, corporate governance is led by a board comprised of directors elected by the state or federal government with additional directors elected by non-government shareholders. Brazilian enterprises with state ownership are concentrated in the energy, electricity generation and distribution, transportation, and banking sectors. Many of these firms are also publically traded companies on the Brazilian and other stock exchanges.

The GOB created a number of new state-owned enterprises in 2012. In August, the Planning and Logistics Company (EPL) was founded to oversee the development and integration of various forms of transportation, including the concessions for roads and railways. The EPL is also responsible for the development of the bullet train project that will connect Sao Paulo, Campinas, and Rio de Janeiro.

Also in August, President Rousseff signed a provisional measure (MP 564) which would allow for the creation of a state-owned enterprise for reinsurance, the Brazilian Management Agency of Funds and Guarantees, known as "Segurobras." The purpose of the company would be to provide government-backed reinsurance for large infrastructure projects, such as for World Cup and Olympics construction, which do not have full coverage in the private market.

In December, the GOB created Infraero Serviços, a state-owned company mandated to manage the network of regional airports. The GOB intends for Infraero Serviços to eventually co-manage the airports along with a private sector concessionaire.

Corporate Social Responsibility

Most state-owned and private sector corporations of any significant size in Brazil pursue corporate social responsibility (CSR) activities. Many corporations support local education, health and other programs in the communities where they have a presence. Brazilian consumers, especially the local citizenry where a corporation has or is planning a local presence, expect CSR activity. It is not uncommon for corporate officials to meet with community members prior to building a new plant or factory to review what types of local services the corporation will commit to providing. Foreign and local enterprises in Brazil often advance United Nations Development Program (UNDP) Millennium Development Goals (MDGs) as part of their CSR activity, and will cite their local contributions to MDGs such as universal primary education and environmental sustainability.

The U.S. diplomatic mission in Brazil supports American business CSR activities through the +Unidos Group (Mais Unidos), a group of more than 100 American companies established in Brazil. Additional information on how the partnership supports public and private alliances in Brazil can be found on its website: www.maisunidos.org.

The private sector in Brazil is increasingly engaging in public-private partnerships for investments in environmental and socio-economic development initiatives. Currently Mais Unidos, in partnership with USAID, has two joint projects in the areas of education and environment. The education/English language project, Mais Opportunidades, has been operating in Rio de Janeiro since 2011 with the support from the Rio de Janeiro state government, and will benefit disadvantaged youth. The environment project, Mais Unidos for the Amazon, contributes to preserve the biodiversity of the region.

Political Violence

Strikes and demonstrations occur occasionally in urban areas and may cause temporary disruption to public transportation. Widespread public sector strikes by federal government employees in Brasilia in 2012 remained peaceful. Although U.S. citizens have traditionally not been targeted during such events, U.S. citizens traveling or residing in Brazil are advised to take common-sense precautions and avoid any large gatherings or any other event where crowds have congregated to demonstrate or protest. For the latest U.S.

State Department guidance on travel in Brazil, please consult www.travel.state.gov.

Corruption

In 2012, Brazil ranked 69th (out of 174 countries) in Transparency International's Corruption Perceptions Index. In South America, Brazil ranked behind Chile and Uruguay, and ranked ahead of Colombia, Peru, Argentina, Suriname, Bolivia, Ecuador, Guyana, Paraguay and Venezuela. With regard to major emerging economies in the BRICS grouping, Brazil ranked ahead of China (80th), India (94th), and Russia (133rd), and tied with South Africa (69th).

Corruption scandals are a regular feature of Brazilian political life. Politics in 2012 were dominated by Penal Case 470, more commonly known as the "Mensalão" case, under which defendants including some past and present members of the Brazilian Congress were found guilty of participating in a pay-for-votes scheme. A former president of the Chamber of Deputies, former President Lula's chief of staff, and 24 other current and former public officials were convicted in the highly-followed trial, which was viewed as a positive step in the fight against corruption. In her first year in office, 2011, President Rousseff dismissed six ministers after allegations of diversion of public funds and/or influence peddling in their ministries. Authorities have conducted corruption investigations involving politicians from both opposition and government coalition parties over the course of the last several years.

Brazil is a signatory to the Organization for Economic Cooperation and Development (OECD) Anti-Bribery Convention. It was one of the founders, along with the United States, of the intergovernmental Open Government Partnership, which seeks to help governments increase transparency. Brazil has laws, regulations and penalties to combat corruption, but their effectiveness is inconsistent. Bribery is illegal, and a bribe by a local company to a foreign official is a criminal act. A company cannot deduct a bribe to a foreign official from its taxes. While federal government authorities generally investigate allegations of corruption, there are inconsistencies in the level of enforcement among individual states. Corruption has been reported to be problematic in business dealings with some authorities, particularly at the municipal level. U.S. companies operating in Brazil are subject to the U.S. Foreign Corrupt Practices Act.

Bilateral Investment Agreements

Brazil does not have a Bilateral Investment Treaty with the United States. In the 1990's Brazil signed BITs with Belgium and Luxembourg, Chile, Cuba, Denmark, Finland, France, Germany, Italy, the Republic of Korea, the Netherlands, Portugal, Switzerland, the United Kingdom and Venezuela, but none of these have been approved by the Brazilian Congress. Brazil also has not approved the Mercosur investment protocol.

Brazil does not have a double taxation treaty with the United States, but it does have such treaties with 24 other countries, including, among others, Japan, France, Italy, the Netherlands, Canada and Argentina. Brazil signed a Tax Information Exchange Agreement with the United States in March 2007 that passed the Brazilian Chamber of Deputies in December 2009 and currently awaits action in the Brazilian Senate.

OPIC and Other Investment Insurance Programs

Programs of the Overseas Private Investment Corporation (OPIC) are fully available, and activity has increased in recent years. The size of OPIC's exposure in Brazil may occasionally limit its capacity for new coverage. Brazil has been a member of the Multilateral Investment Guarantee Agency (MIGA) since 1992.

Labor

The Brazilian Ministry of Finance estimates that 19.3 million jobs were created in Brazil from January 2003 to October 2012. In 2012, a net 1.3 million jobs were created, compared to 1.9 million in 2011.

According to a 2011 Brazilian Institute of Geography and Statistics (IBGE) report, the Brazilian labor force is 92.5 million workers strong. Roughly 58% were located in the services sector, 15% in agriculture, 21% in the construction and manufacturing.

Brazil has signed on to a large number of International Labor Organization (ILO) conventions. Brazil is party to the U.N. Convention on the Rights of the Child and major ILO conventions concerning the prohibition of child labor, forced labor and discrimination.

The labor code is highly detailed and relatively generous to workers. Formal sector workers are guaranteed 30 days of annual leave and severance pay in the case of dismissal without cause. Brazilian employers are required to pay a "thirteenth month" of salary to employees at the end of the year. Brazil also has a system of labor courts that are charged with resolving routine cases involving unfair dismissal, working conditions, salary disputes, and other grievances. Labor courts have the power to impose an agreement on employers and unions if negotiations break down and either side appeals to the court system. As a result, labor courts routinely are called upon to determine wages and working conditions in industries across the country. The system is tantamount to compulsory arbitration and does not encourage collective bargaining. In recent years, however, both labor and management have become more flexible and collective bargaining has assumed greater relevance.

The Ministry of Labor estimates that there are nearly 15,000 labor unions in Brazil, but Ministry officials note that these figures are inexact. Labor unions, especially in sectors such as metalworking and banking, tend to be well-organized and aggressive in advocating for wages and working conditions and account for approximately 19 percent of the official workforce according to a recent IBGE release. Strikes occur periodically, particularly among public sector unions. Unions in various sectors engage in industry-wide collective bargaining negotiations mandated by federal regulation. While some labor organizations and their leadership operate independently of the government and of political parties, others are viewed as closely associated with political parties.

In firms employing three or more persons, Brazilian nationals must constitute at least two-thirds of all employees and receive at least two-thirds of total payroll. Foreign specialists in fields where Brazilians are unavailable are not counted in calculating the one-third permitted for non-Brazilians.

The IBGE statistical agency estimated unemployment in the major metropolitan areas as of December 2012 at 4.6 percent. With low unemployment, there is currently a shortage of highly-skilled workers. Unemployment levels range significantly across regions.

IBGE reports show that real wages have trended higher in recent years. The average monthly wage in Brazil's six largest cities was around R$1,787.70 in October 2012 (approximately USD 880 based on average exchange rates for that month). The minimum monthly wage has regularly been increased in recent years from R$380 in 2007 to R$671 (approximately USD 335) in 2013. Earnings vary significantly by region and industry, and there is significant, though gradually declining, income inequality between Brazil's poor and wealthy.

Employer federations, supported by mandatory fees based on payroll, play a significant role in both public policy and labor relations. Each state has its own federation, which reports to the National Confederation of Industries (CNI), headquartered in Brasilia.

Foreign Trade Zones/Free Trade Zones

The federal government has granted tax benefits for certain free trade zones. Most of these free trade zones aim to attract investment to the country's relatively underdeveloped North and Northeast regions. The most prominent of these is the Manaus Free Trade Zone, in Amazonas State, which has attracted significant foreign investment, including from U.S. companies. According to SUFRAMA, the Brazilian federal agency responsible for the economic development of the Amazon region, for the eleven months ending November 2012, the companies of the Manaus industrial area generated USD 32.8 billion in revenues, an increase of 22.6 percent over the same period in 2011. In October 2011, President Rousseff signed a constitutional amendment which extends Manaus's status as an industrial zone for another 50 years.

Foreign Direct Investment and Foreign Direct Investment Statistics

According to the Central Bank's most recent foreign-capital census (2010), the United States had the largest share of accumulated foreign-capital stock in Brazil, with 18.0 percent of the total. Spain had 14.7 percent, Belgium 8.7 percent, and Brazil 8.3 percent. Net foreign direct investment inflows between the years 2006 to 2011 have amounted to about USD 377 billion, after subtracting depreciation and capital repatriation.

According to the UN, Brazil was in 2012 the fourth largest destination of foreign direct investment, trailing only the United States, China, and Hong Kong. The same criteria placed Brazil in fifth in 2011 and seventh in 2010.

According to data published by the Central Bank, FDI inflows to Brazil are anticipated to have reached more than USD 65 billion in 2012, a figure 2 percent lower than 2011. Additionally, according to the U.S. Bureau of

Economic Analysis, the stock of FDI from the United States in Brazil was USD 71.1 billion as of the end of 2011.

Total FDI flows into Brazil as a Percentage of Brazilian GDP

Year	FDI (USD Billions)	Percentage of GDP
2012	65.3	2.7*
2011	66.7	2.7
2010	48.4	2.3
2009	25.9	1.6
2008	45.1	2.8
2007	34.6	2.6
2006	18.8	1.7
2005	15.1	1.7
2004	18.1	2.7
2003	10.1	1.8

*Estimated.
Source: Central Bank of Brazil.

For more information on investing in Brazil, contact the Brazilian Trade and Investment Promotion Agency, ApexBrasil: http://www.apexbrasil.com.br.

In: Brazil, Russia, India, China, and South Africa   ISBN: 978-1-62618-627-9
Editor: Sandra C. Owens   © 2013 Nova Science Publishers, Inc.

Chapter 2

2013 INVESTMENT CLIMATE STATEMENT: RUSSIA*

Bureau of Economic and Business Affairs

OPENNESS TO, AND RESTRICTIONS UPON, FOREIGN INVESTMENT

Russian President Vladimir Putin has stated that improving the investment climate in Russia and increasing foreign direct investment (FDI) is a priority for his tenure as President. This commitment led to a variety of reforms in 2012 that sought to reduce administrative barriers and provide incentives for foreign businesses looking to invest in Russia. The capstone of this commitment was Russia's accession to the World Trade Organization (WTO) in August of 2012, reducing tariffs across the board and securing a variety of market-opening acts by the Russian government. Russia continues to promote the use of high-tech parks, special economic zones and industrial clusters which offer additional tax and infrastructure incentives to attract investment. One of Putin's stated goals, to move Russia from 120th (in 2010) to 20th on the World Bank's Doing Business Index by 2020, saw incremental progress with Russia climbing to 112th in the 2012 publication. Russia's continued engagement in the accession process to the Organization for Economic

---

* This is an edited, reformatted and augmented version of Bureau of Economic and Business Affairs publication, dated February 2013.

Cooperation and Development (OECD) could also lead to greater market access for foreign investors.

Despite these positive changes, investing in the Russian market still requires that firms navigate a complicated and fluid set of challenges ranging from complex and burdensome regulatory processes to corruption that marks both political and judicial structures. The Russian economy was impacted by the global economic slowdown and the 2008-2009 financial crisis but has quickly rebounded thanks to high energy prices and use of two sovereign wealth funds to inject capital into domestic markets. Russia's GDP growth forecast of 3.6 percent in 2013 is a healthy figure when compared to the expected continuation of economic contraction in Europe, slow growth in the United States, and deceleration in China. However, Russia continues to be particularly vulnerable to global energy prices and continued weakness in the European economy, as the EU represents more than 50 percent of Russia's total trade volume. According to the United Nations Conference on Trade and Development (UNCTAD) 2012 World Investment Report, Russia saw FDI flows grow 22 percent, reaching USD 53 billion in 2011, its third-highest level ever recorded. In addition, in 2011, according to Ernst & Young's 2012 Russia Attractiveness Survey, Russia was the premier destination for investment in Central and Eastern Europe. This Survey combined analysis of statistical data with a survey of 208 global executives, 135 of whom do business in Russia. According to the survey, 19 percent of international investors considered Russia to be one of the most attractive regions of the world; this was up 8 percent from the previous year's results. According to the Central Bank of Russia, in 1H 2012, FDI into Russia reached USD16.2 billion, with manufacturers and the financial industry receiving most of the money (the most recent numbers available). The Economic Development Ministry forecasts that 2012 FDI in Russia will exceed the 2011 level and will likely reach about USD 60 billion.

Prime Minister Medvedev is particularly committed to building a strong high technology sector in Russia. The country's solid base of expertise in the scientific and mathematics fields, combined with a sizable market and an economy growing faster than most others in the region, have helped entice a series of U.S. firms to make investments in Russia. Roughly a dozen U.S. companies and organizations already have announced their intention to invest in the Skolkovo Innovation Center, Russia's high-tech cluster in Moscow's outskirts modeled on the example of Silicon Valley.

While a legal structure exists to support foreign investors, the laws are not always enforced in practice. The 1991 Investment Code and 1999 Law on

Foreign Investment guarantee that foreign investors enjoy rights equal to those of Russian investors, although some industries have limits on foreign ownership (see Establishment section). Russia has sought to enhance consultation mechanisms with international businesses, including through the Foreign Investment Advisory Council whose members are CEOs of large companies, regarding the impact of the country's legislation and regulations on the business and investment climate. Russia has a system of Investment Ombudsmen at the federal and regional levels. In June 2012, President Putin created the position of Ombudsman for Entrepreneur's Rights, designed to be an additional measure of protection and advocacy for entrepreneurs. In December 2012, the State Duma approved the Business Ombudsman Law in its first reading and is expected to adopt the bill in the first half of 2013. Still, the country's investment dispute resolution mechanisms remain a work in progress, and at present can seem non-transparent and unpredictable (see Dispute Settlement section).

Russian government officials have repeatedly stressed that foreign investment and technology transfer are critical to Russia's economic modernization. At the same time, the government continues to limit foreign investment in sectors deemed to have strategic significance for national defense and state security via the Strategic Sectors Law of 2008. The law originally specified 42 activities that require government approval for foreign investment. Foreign investors wishing to increase or gain ownership above certain thresholds need to seek prior approval from a government commission headed by Russia's Prime Minister. The 2012 addition of Russian privately-held internet company Yandex to the strategic companies list highlights the broad interpretation of what is required to protect state security and national defense. However, there have been some adjustments to the list. Notably in 2011, Russia amended the law to simplify the approval process and narrow the range of potential investments requiring formal review. While the Commission has approved 129 of 137 applications for foreign investment since 2008, the number of transactions approved with conditions has been increasing significantly. Statements made by key Russian officials in November of 2012 suggest the government will take additional action to roll back administrative barriers to foreign investment in Russian strategic companies. The Federal Antimonopoly Service (FAS) prepared various amendments, still awaiting approval by the State Duma, intended to simplify the procedures for state supervision of foreign investment in Russian strategic companies and to eliminate ambiguities in the interpretation and application of existing legislative provisions. (see Regulatory Transparency)

The share of the private sector in Russia's GDP continued to decrease in 2012, falling to 50 percent from 60 percent in 2006, according to the Russian Ministry of the Economy. The government also continues to hold significant blocks of shares in many privatized enterprises. In an effort to increase market forces in the economy and raise revenue for the federal budget, in 2009 the government began considering more ambitious privatization of strategic enterprises. In October 2010, the Russian Cabinet approved a major Privatization Plan to sell an estimated $60 billion of government stakes in about 1000 companies (out of a total of 6,467 companies with some government ownership). This has been superseded by President Putin's May 2012 Privatization Plan. To date, treatment of foreign investment in new privatizations has been inconsistent; foreign participation has often been confined to limited positions. Subsequently, many have faced problems with inadequate protection for minority shareholders and corporate governance. Potential foreign investors are advised to work directly and closely with appropriate local, regional, and federal agencies that exercise ownership or authority over companies whose shares they may want to acquire. (See State-Owned Enterprises) In September of 2012, the United States and Russia signed a new bilateral visa agreement which extended the validity of a tourist visa to 36 months for both American and Russian travelers. This agreement also reduced the documentary requirements for Americans applying for a visa and eliminated the need for an invitation letter in most cases. The process for the approval and renewal of visas and residence permits for foreign businessmen and investors remains cumbersome with numerous documentary requirements. Additionally, there are regulations in specific industries that require a certain percentage of staff be Russian citizens, which may have a negative impact on foreign investors. The situation is improving, however. As part of Russia's efforts to encourage investment in innovation sectors, the GOR has eased the regulations on visas and residence permits for "highly-skilled" workers, and eliminated yearly quotas for foreign workers who fall into this category (defined by salary, position and education level). Potential investors are advised to consult the *State Department's Country-Specific Information on travel to Russia,* which includes the latest information on Russian visas.

Corruption remains a major challenge for Russia. Targeted efforts in 2012 to root out corruption by public officials and within business transactions led to widely reported investigations in the Ministry of Defense and the Ministry of Agriculture. Russia's ranking improved 10 spots to 133rd in Transparency International's 2012 Corruption Perceptions Index (CPI). The National Anti-Corruption Plan for 2012–2013 contains guidance and recommendations for the government on counteracting corruption, including the establishment of a legal framework for lobbying and increasing the transparency of state officials' personal finances and acceptance of gifts. Specifically, the bill will require all civil servants to declare large expenditures or face termination. These officials must also present information on the expenditures of their spouses and children if the expenditures involve acquisitions of land, vehicles or securities. Expenditures that do not match the declared income will be investigated by law enforcement agencies. If an individual fails to prove that the property in question was acquired legally, the property will be confiscated and turned over to the state. Bribing a public official has been illegal in Russia since May 2011 (see Corruption section).

Global Benchmarks

The following table includes the most recent data from indices measuring the investment and business climate in Russia:

Measure	Year	Index/Ranking
Transparency International Corruption Index	2012	28 – 133 of 176 countries
Heritage Economic Freedom	2012	50.5 – 144 of 184 countries
World Bank Doing Business	2013	112 of 185 economies
Fiscal Policy (IMF World Economic Outlook)	2011 (est.)	Government net annual borrowing: 1.11% of GDP
Trade Policy (Heritage Economic Freedom)	2012	68.2 (moderately free)
Business Start Up (World Bank Doing Business)	2013	101 of 185economies
Land Rights Access (World Bank Doing Business) Freedom Rating (Freedom House)	2013 2013	Construction Permits: 178 of 185 economies Registering Property: 46 of 185economies 5.5 out of 7 (scale of 1-7, 1 being the best) Status: Not Free Political Rights: 6 Civil Liberties: 5

Currency Conversion and Capital Transfers

While the ruble is the only legal tender in Russia, companies and individuals generally face no significant difficulty in obtaining foreign exchange. Only authorized banks may carry out foreign currency transactions but finding a licensed bank is not difficult. According to currency control laws, the Central Bank retains the right to impose restrictions on the purchase of foreign currency, including the requirement that the transaction be completed through a special account. The Central Bank does not require security deposits on foreign exchange purchases. Russia has no capital controls and there are no barriers to remitting investment returns abroad, including dividends, interest, and returns of capital. Nonetheless, investors should seek expert advice at the time of an investment.

Currency controls exist on all transactions that require customs clearance, which in Russia applies to both import and export transactions and certain loans. A business must open a "deal passport" with the authorized Russian bank through which it will receive and service the transaction or loan. A "deal passport" is a set of documents that importers and exporters provide to authorized banks which enable the bank to monitor payments with respect to the transaction or loan and to report the corporation's compliance with currency control regulations to the Central Bank. (Russia's regulations regarding deal passports are prescribed under Instructions of the Central Bank of Russia number 117-I of June 15, 2004.) In early 2011, the Central Bank of Russia expanded the list of grounds under which a deal passport does not have to be submitted. The Central Bank adopted Instruction number 1238-I on June 4th, 2012, which states "On order of submission by residents and nonresidents to authorized banks of documents and information relative to conducting of currency operations, order of deal passport formalization as well as order of currency operations' registration by authorized banks and control for their execution". One of the innovations suggested by the Instruction is an opportunity to file notifications on currency operations by an authorized bank. Previously, the parties involved in the transaction had to file the notification, themselves. Though the notification is an important element of Russia's currency controls, under current regulations, basic transaction such as direct debiting from foreign currency accounts held by Russian residents are precluded. Once this Instruction enters into force, it is anticipated that this type of transaction will be permitted. Another improvement is the ability of the resident legal entity to the contract (loan agreement), to transfer formalization of the deal passport and currency operations relating to that contract, to its branch.

Expropriation and Compensation

The 1991 Investment Code prohibits the nationalization of foreign investments, except following legislative action and where deemed to be in the national interest. Such nationalizations may be appealed to Russian courts, and the investor must be adequately and promptly compensated. At the sub-federal level, expropriation has occasionally been a problem, as has local government interference and a lack of enforcement of court rulings protecting investors.

Dispute Settlement

Russia has a body of conflicting, overlapping, and frequently changing laws, decrees and regulations, which complicates the environment for dispute resolution. In an attempt to address these challenges, First Deputy Prime Minister Shuvalov in 2010 was designated "Investment Ombudsman" which entails coordinating and overseeing efforts to improve the business and investment climate, including the protection of foreign and domestic investors. In 2011, President Medvedev appointed additional Investment Ombudsmen in each Federal District to perform similar roles at the regional level. The government has also encouraged international business leaders, as part of their work in the Foreign Investment Advisory Council, to participate in the discussion of dispute resolution mechanisms and individual commercial disputes. While these steps offer some promise, overall, the country's investment dispute mechanisms remain underdeveloped and largely non-transparent. In 2012, President Putin named "Business Russia" leader Boris Titov as Ombudsman for entrepreneurs' rights. Titov's remit includes advocating for business rights in court and requesting suspension of official actions if a business feels its rights were violated.

Independent dispute resolution in Russia can be difficult to obtain since the judicial system is still developing. Courts are sometimes subject to political pressure. According to numerous reports, corruption in the judicial system is widespread and takes many forms, ranging from bribes of judges and prosecutors to fabrication of evidence. Corruption likely does not play a role in the vast majority of cases, most of which involve relatively low stakes. A law enacted in late 2008 as part of President Medvedev's anti-corruption initiative requires that judges disclose their incomes and real estate assets, including those owned by their spouses and minor children.

Another component of President Medvedev's anti-corruption initiative included a series of amendments to the Code of Criminal Procedure – in 2008, 2009, and 2010 – to limit pre-trial detention of individuals accused of economic crimes. Implementation of these reforms has yielded mixed results. Prosecutors have sometimes avoided them by charging defendants under articles technically not covered by the amendments and judges have sometimes refused to apply them. Nevertheless, available statistics reveal a substantial decrease in the number of pre-trial detentions in cases involving economic crimes since the legislation was passed.

Commercial courts are required by law to decide business disputes relatively quickly, and many cases are decided on the basis of written evidence and little or no live testimony of witnesses. The commercial court workload is dominated by relatively simple non-contentious cases involving the collection of debts between firms and disputes with the taxation and customs authorities, pension fund, and other state organs. Tax-paying firms often prevail in their disputes with the government in court. The number of routine cases limits the time available to decide more complex cases. Many observers believe that over the twenty year period that the commercial court system has existed, its judges have grown more competent and better at writing decisions. Many lawyers nonetheless report that due to insufficient training, especially in complex business disputes, many judges often make poorly reasoned or simply incorrect decisions. Execution of court decisions is often problematic. Few firms pay judgments against them voluntarily and rumors of corruption concerning bailiffs, who are charged with enforcing decisions, are frequent, although hard evidence is scarce.

Federal Law 262, in effect since mid-2010, requires courts to publish their decisions online and otherwise make information about their activities publicly available. All Russian courts now have websites, which generally include a schedule of cases to be heard, the name of the judge, the location of the court, form documents that can be used by prospective litigants, and copies of decisions. Personal information is expunged before case decisions are posted online. The better websites allow citizens to calculate filing fees and search for analogous decisions. The commercial courts have played a leadership role in providing information online and using information technology. Electronic filing allows citizens to sign up to receive e-mail notifications of developments in cases of interest to them. NGOs have rated the compliance of courts with their obligations under the law and found that the information provided varies greatly in quality from one region to another, but have noted a willingness by some courts to respond to queries and criticisms by improving their sites. Although there are gaps and failures to provide information, overall judicial transparency has increased since the law took effect in 2010.

Many attorneys refer Western clients who have investment or trade disputes in Russia to international arbitration in Stockholm or to courts abroad. A 1997 Russian law allows foreign arbitration awards to be enforced in Russia, even if there is no reciprocal treaty between Russia and the country where the order was issued. Russia is a member of the International Center for the Settlement of Investment Disputes (ICSID) and accepts binding international arbitration. Russia is also a signatory to the 1958 New York Convention on the Recognition and Enforcement of Foreign Arbitral Awards (UNCITRAL). However, international arbitral awards still require Russian courts to enforce awards and bailiffs to attach assets; these have yet to become consistently effective enforcers of court judgments, whether domestic or international.

As noted above, commercial disputes between business entities are heard in the commercial court system. That court system has special procedures for the seizure of property before trial, such that it cannot be disposed of before the court has heard the claim, as well as for the enforcement of financial awards through the banks. Additionally, the International Commercial Arbitration Court at the Russian Chamber of Commerce and Industry will hear claims if both parties agree to refer disputes there. A similar arbitration court has been established in St. Petersburg. As with international arbitral procedures, the weakness in the Russian arbitration system lies in the enforcement of decisions.

As per Federal Law of December 2011, a specialized court for intellectual property (IP) disputes is schedule to open in early 2013. This court, embedded in the system of arbitration (commercial) courts, will hear cases on intellectual property rights (IPR), including those challenging statutory instruments on IP, in the first instance and cassation. In September 2012 the Higher Qualification Board of Judges (a body within the Russian judicial corps responsible for nominating judges to be further appointed by the President) nominated 20 judges to form the new IPR Court, and the Chief Judge of the IPR Court was appointed by the President in December 2012.

Former President Medvedev encouraged widespread adoption of alternative dispute resolution (ADR) to help courts handle their caseloads and to provide citizens with speedier and cheaper methods of resolving legal disputes. In January 2011, a new law took effect that authorizes the use of mediation in various kinds of disputes, including commercial ones, and provides for the confidentiality of mediation proceedings and for their enforceability in court. Although there are still issues concerning implementation, this represents an important step towards further development of ADR in Russia.

The level of professionalism in the legal bar, including in the realm of corporate compliance, continues to grow. While significant quality disparities reportedly still exist between large international firms with Russia offices and indigenous Russian firms, there are indications that continued joint trainings and other professional interactions are slowly improving the quality of local legal support for the business community.

Performance Requirements and Incentives

Performance requirements are not generally imposed by Russian law and are not widely included as part of private contracts in Russia. However, they have appeared in the agreements of large multinational companies investing in natural resources and in production-sharing legislation. There are no formal requirements for offsets in foreign investments. Since approval for investments in Russia frequently depends on relationships with government officials and on a firm's demonstration of its commitment to the Russian market, this may result in offsets in practice.

The Central Bank of Russia has imposed caps on foreign employees in foreign banks. The ratio of Russian employees in a subsidiary of a foreign bank is set at no less than 75 percent; if the executive of the subsidiary is a non-resident, at least 50 percent of the bank's managing body are to be Russians.

Right to Private Ownership and Establishment

Both foreign and domestic legal entities may establish, purchase, and dispose of businesses in Russia, except in certain sectors that are regarded as affecting national security.

The Russian government limits foreign investment in sectors deemed to have strategic significance for national defense and state security via the Strategic Sectors Law of 2008. The law originally specified 42 activities that require government approval for foreign investment. Foreign investors wishing to increase or gain ownership above certain thresholds need to seek prior approval from a government commission headed by Russia's Prime Minister. The 2012 addition of Russian privately-held internet company Yandex to the strategic companies list highlights the broad interpretation of what is required to protect state security and national defense. However, there have been some adjustments to the list. Notably in 2011, Russia amended the law to simplify the approval process and narrow the range of potential investments requiring formal review by the Commission. With respect to extractive industries, government approval was previously required for foreign ownership above a 10 percent threshold for companies operating subsoil plots of "federal significance." The November 2011 reforms raised the threshold to 25 percent, a move that experts predict will greatly reduce the number of cases considered. While the Commission has approved 129 of 137 applications for foreign investment since 2008, the number of transactions approved with conditions has been increasing significantly.

Protection of Property Rights

Real Estate: The Constitution and a 1993 presidential decree give Russian citizens general rights to own, inherit, lease, mortgage, and sell real property. Foreigners enjoy similar rights with certain restrictions, notably with respect to the ownership of farmland and areas located near federal borders. Mortgage legislation enacted in 2004 facilitates the process for lenders to evict homeowners who do not stay current in their mortgage payments. Thus far this law has been successfully implemented and generally effective. Mortgage lending is in its initial stages, and after a sharp contraction in 2008-09, the total value of mortgages in Russia is around three percent of GDP. In January – November 2012, mortgage lending grew by 40 percent over the same period of 2011, with new issuances amounting to USD 32 billion in the first eleven months of the year.

IPR: In Russia, the protection of intellectual property rights (IPR) is enforced on the basis of civil, administrative, criminal or customs legislation. The Civil Code sets up the level of compensation for IPR infringement and/or incurred damages for copyright, trademarks and geographical indications. The Code of Administrative Offenses concerns IPR infractions that violate public or private interest or rights, but do not meet the criteria of the Criminal Code. An administrative investigation may be initiated at the request of an IPR owner or by law enforcement authorities (police or customs) suspecting possible IPR infringement. Administrative cases are dealt with by general jurisdiction courts or state arbitration (commercial) courts that have jurisdiction over economic disputes. The IPR provisions of the Criminal Code apply to large-scale infringements of copyright, patent and trademark rights that cause gross damages, as defined by the Criminal Code.

Enforcement: In recent years, Russia made significant progress in improving the legislative environment and legal framework for IPR protection. Russia passed amendments to Part IV of the Civil Code for compliance with the Trade-Related Aspects of Intellectual Property (TRIPs) agreement, amended its Customs Code to include ex-officio authority for Russian Customs officials, and amended the Law on Circulation of Medicines to provide for 6 years of regulatory data protection effective as of Russia's accession to the WTO in August 2012. However, implementation and enforcement thereof is subject to the respective regulations and corresponding bylaws, which are yet to be developed. Additionally, a law adopted in December 2011 laid the foundation for the establishment of a Russian IPR Court within Russia's system of commercial courts by February 2013.

Copyright violations (films, videos, sound recordings, computer software) remain a serious problem, particularly in the online environment. Although dwarfed in volume by pirated products online, legitimate DVD sales are on the rise, thanks in part to cheaper legitimate products, a growing consumer preference for high quality goods, and increased law enforcement action against pirates. Local representatives of the entertainment and software industries have also reported marginal declines in levels of piracy. Russian police on occasion carry out end-user raids against businesses using pirated products. However, at times, police have used IPR enforcement as a tactic to elicit bribes or harass NGOs.

Bankruptcy: Russia has had a law providing for bankruptcy of enterprises since the early 1990s. Law enforcement officials, however, tend to view bankruptcy with suspicion and reported 500 cases of financial crime involving bankruptcy in 2011. In November 2012, the State Duma passed in its first reading (three readings required for passage) a personal bankruptcy bill. The bill states that a citizen who finds himself in financial difficulty can submit a bankruptcy statement to the court. The court may then grant the individual the right to pay the debt in installments for a term of up to five years. An individual with debts exceeding 50,000 rubles (USD 1,576) and whose arrears amount to three months can be declared bankrupt. In this case, the individual cannot apply for a bank loan without citing his bankruptcy for the five years after his bankruptcy status was declared. The individual is then given six months to come up with a debt restricting plan subject to the approval of both the creditors and the court. Once the plan is approved, all late payment fees and penalties will be waived and assets unfrozen. Only in the case of a person who has no assets and no income may the debt be completely written off. The bill also stipulates a ban on declaring oneself bankrupt more than once in five years. The Duma is expected to approve the bill in the first half of 2013 with provisions possibly coming into effect in 2014.

Transparency of the Regulatory System

Russia's legal system remains in a state of flux, with various parts of the government continuing to implement new regulations and decrees on a broad array of topics, including the tax code and requirements related to regulatory and inspection bodies. Negotiations and contracts for commercial transactions, as well as due diligence processes, are complex and protracted. Investors must do careful research to ensure that each contract fully conforms to Russian law. Contracts must likewise seek to protect the foreign partner against contingencies that often arise. Keeping up with legislative changes, presidential decrees, and government resolutions is a challenging task. Uneven implementation of laws creates further complications; various officials, branches of government, and jurisdictions interpret and apply regulations inconsistently and the decisions of one may be overruled or contested by another. As a result, reaching final agreement with local political and economic authorities can be a long and burdensome process. Companies should be prepared to allocate sufficient funds to engage local legal counsel to set up their commercial operations in Russia.

Taxes: Russia's tax system has recently undergone major changes. The Russian government has brought its tax legislation into line with OECD requirements, which has simplified the system, and prevents double taxation on transfer prices. Businesses nonetheless continue to raise concerns regarding audits. Multiple audits, repeated requests for documentation, and technical weaknesses of some claims have been identified as serious impediments to the conduct of business. The Council of the Russian Chamber of Commerce and Industry's Working Group of Tax Experts has predicted that in 2013-14 tax audits will increase, be exercised even more strictly, with larger assessments, as the system of incentives for tax inspectors was revised in 2012 to take into account the amount of additional tax accruals resulting from tax audits (2011 tax audits brought RUB 4.5 million to federal coffers). Russia's new Law on Transfer Pricing entered into force on January 1, 2012, with certain provisions scheduled to be phased in by 2014. Some experts caution that once all provisions are enacted in 2014, additional disputes with tax authorities might flare up.

Public Comment: All draft laws that go through the Russian Duma are published on the Duma's website. Sometimes, but not consistently, ministries and other Russian government bodies also publish proposed legislation (including draft laws, government decrees and regulations) on their websites. Russia's Open Government initiative aims to provide more transparency and governmental accountability to Russian citizens by creating opportunities for public comment on a wide range of initiatives. Russian Ministries have become more active in seeking input from industry experts and business groups, including the Foreign Investment Advisory Council, when developing business-related laws and regulations. Some NGOs claim Open Government is largely a public relations effort that will result in few substantive changes in decision- making. However, Russia is in the initial stages of this initiative and it is too soon to come to a conclusion on the efficacy of the program.

Strategic Sectors: Statements made by key Russian officials in November of 2012 suggest the government will take additional action to roll back administrative barriers to foreign investment in Russian strategic companies. The Federal Antimonopoly Service (FAS) has prepared various amendments, still awaiting approval by the State Duma, intended to simplify the procedures for state supervision of foreign investment in Russian strategic companies and to eliminate ambiguities in the interpretation and application of existing legislative provisions. The proposed amendments include the following: (1) removal of food and beverage production from the list of strategic activities involving the use of infectious agents (e.g. cultured bacteria in yogurt production). FAS is considering similar revisions to exempt certain entities involving selected activities (e.g foreign banks vis-a-vis distribution and servicing of encryption devices required for their operations); (2) eliminating the need for prior approval by the Government Commission for certain share increases or transactions in cases where the foreign investors hold 75 percent or more of a Russian strategic company's shares; (3) eliminating the need for prior approval for intra-group transactions by foreign investors controlled by the same entity; (4) allowance of automatic permit extensions for foreign investors already holding a permit (typically with a 2-year term) to invest in a strategic enterprise; (5) elimination of the need for government approval for acquisitions by Russian-controlled purchasers from foreign-controlled sellers (currently, only Russian-to-Russian transactions are exempt, but not acquisitions by Russian-controlled purchasers from foreign-controlled sellers); (6) clearer rules on state supervision and approval of transactions involving the placement of securities of Russian strategic companies (including depositary receipts) on stock exchanges, including foreign stock exchanges.

Capital Markets and Portfolio Investment

The Russian banking system remains relatively small, with RUB 43.2 trillion (USD 1.4 trillion) in aggregate net assets as of October 1, 2012. Although Russia has roughly 1000 banks, the sector is dominated by state-owned banks, particularly Sberbank and VTB. The six largest banks (in terms of assets) in Russia are state-controlled, and the top five held 50.9% of all bank assets in Russia as of November 1, 2012. The successful implementation of the Deposit Insurance System in 2004 has proved a critical psychological boon to the banking sector, reflected in the overall growth of deposits. Despite measured progress, the Russian banking system is not yet efficiently performing its basic role of financial intermediary (i.e., taking deposits and lending to business and individuals). At the beginning of 2012, aggregate assets of the banking sector amounted to just 76.3% of GDP and aggregate capital was just 9.6% of GDP. Russia's banking sector has nearly recovered from the economic crisis, with corporate loan growth reaching 17.1% and retail loan growth 42.7% in the 12 months running to November 1, 2012. The Bank of Russia considers the latter too rapid and is taking measures to restrain it. The share within Russia's banking sector of non-performing and troubled loans, which during the 2008-2009 financial crisis increased substantially, stabilized in 2010 at around 20% and began to slowly decline in the second half of 2011, such that in November 2012 it was less than 16%.

Russia's two main stock exchanges – the Russian Trading System (RTS) and the Moscow Interbank Currency Exchange (MICEX) – merged in December 2011. The MICEX-RTS bourse plans for an initial public offering (IPO), possibly in early 2013. Russian authorities and shareholders of MICEX and RTS believe the merged entity, MICEX-RTS, has the potential to become a global player. However, most large Russian companies currently choose to list their stock in London and elsewhere abroad in order to obtain higher valuations.

The Law on the Securities Market includes definitions of corporate bonds, mutual funds, options, futures, and forwards. Companies offering public shares are required to disclose specific information during the placement process, as well as on a quarterly basis. In addition, the law defines the responsibilities of financial consultants who assist companies with stock offerings and holds them liable for the accuracy of the data presented to shareholders.

Russian financial authorities are attempting to deepen the ruble-denominated domestic debt market to make it more attractive to foreign investors. In December 2011, the Central Bank issued a resolution allowing, effective January 1, 2012, government bonds ("OFZ"s) to be traded outside Russian exchanges (over the counter). Currently, foreign investors wanting to trade domestic bonds must set up local brokerage and custody accounts, a lengthy process that discourages many investors from buying OFZs. Additionally, in October 2012, the Federal Financial Markets Service granted Euroclear Bank, the world's largest settlement system for securities, access to the Central Securities Depository to offer post-trade services for Russian OFZs. The Russian Deputy Finance Minister expressed hope that Russian OFZs would begin trading via Euroclear by early 2013. Hostile takeovers are common in Russia among both foreign and local firms. Private companies' defenses to prevent hostile takeovers relate to all potential hostile takeovers, not just foreign ones.

Russia's financial market suffers from a shortage of private domestic institutional investors. For example, the life insurance market remains underdeveloped, comprising only 6.2% of insurance premium payments. Private pension funds, held back by a public distrust of financial instruments and a lack of tax incentives, currently have an equivalent of USD 17 billion in management, equal to 0.8% of GDP. Pension reform proposals supported by the government in late 2012 would do little to grow the private pension fund industry.

Russia had very high capital outflow (USD 34.6 billion) in early 2012, which later decelerated to average about USD 12 billion per quarter. In January –September 2012, total net private capital outflows were estimated at USD 57.9 billion.

State-Owned Enterprises

The share of the private sector in Russia's gross domestic product (GDP) continued to decrease in 2012, falling to 50 percent from 60 percent in 2006, according to the Russian Ministry of the Economy. The government also continues to hold significant blocks of shares in many privatized enterprises. In an effort to increase market forces in the economy and raise revenue for the federal budget, in 2009 the government began considering more ambitious privatization of state-owned enterprises (SOEs). In October 2010, the Russian Cabinet approved a major Privatization Plan to sell an estimated USD 60 billion of government stakes in about 1000 SOEs (out of a total of 6,467 companies with some government ownership). This has been superseded by President Putin's Privatization Plan, signed in May 2012, which calls for the sale of all state holdings in firms outside the defense and energy industries by 2016. To date, treatment of foreign investment in new privatizations has been inconsistent; foreign participation has often been confined to limited positions. Subsequently, many have faced problems with inadequate protection for minority shareholders and corporate governance. Potential foreign investors are advised to work directly and closely with appropriate local, regional, and federal agencies that exercise ownership or authority over SOEs whose shares they may want to acquire.

President Putin's Privatization Plan contains a preliminary list of companies to be privatized by 2016; the list contains two categories: all non-natural resource sector companies scheduled for privatization over the next 12 to 18 months, and energy companies which will likely see further state consolidation before any equity sale. First Deputy PM Shuvalov has stated publically that the government will not rush privatization, and if market conditions worsen privatization could be further postponed. The October 2012 USD 55 billion purchase by SOE oil giant Rosneft, of 100% of TNK-BP (in which BP received a 20% stake in Rosneft) reflects more a consolidation of assets than any move to lessen State involvement in the economy. Sberbank sold a 7.6% stake in September 2012, leaving the State with 50% plus one share. Bank VTB has expressed plans to sell a 10-25% stake in 2013. Sovkomflot, a shipping group, and Alrosa, a diamond giant, may also sell minority stakes.

Corporate Governance: Despite Russia's ongoing privatization program, the state, whether as majority shareholder in open joint-stock companies or as sole shareholder in "state corporations," continues to play a large role in the Russian economy. (Note: State corporations are 100% owned by the Russian government and operate under special legislation. The Russian economy also features thousands of other companies owned in part or whole by the Russian government that operate under different legal arrangements, such as unitary enterprises and joint stock companies.) Private enterprises are theoretically allowed to compete with SOEs on the same terms and conditions, and in some sectors, including where state ownership is minimal, competition is robust. But in other areas the playing field can be tilted. Issues that hamper efficient operations and fair competition with SOEs include a lack of transparency, lack of independence and unclear responsibilities of boards of directors, misalignment of managers' incentives and company performance, inadequate control mechanisms on managers' total remuneration or their use of assets transferred by the government to the SOE, and minimal disclosure requirements.

SWFs: There are two sovereign wealth funds in Russia: the Reserve Fund (USD 62.08 billion as of January 2013) and the National Wealth Fund (USD 88.59 billion as of January 2013). The Ministry of Finance manages both funds' assets in accordance with established procedures; the Central Bank of Russia acts as operational manager. Both funds are audited by Russia's Chamber of Accounts and the results are reported to the Federal Assembly. The Russian government drew heavily from both funds in 2009 and 2010 to finance bail-out programs for major banks and industries during the global economic crisis.

Corporate Social Responsibility

While far from standard practice, Russian companies are beginning to show an increased level of interest in their reputation as good corporate citizens. When seeking to acquire companies in Western countries or raise capital on international financial markets, Russian companies face international competition and scrutiny, including on corporate social responsibility (CSR) standards. Consequently, most large Russian companies currently have a CSR policy in place, or are developing one, despite the lack of pressure from Russian consumers and shareholders. Russian firms' CSR policies often are now published on corporate websites and detailed in annual reports. These CSR policies and strategies, however, are still in an early stage relative to those of Western counterparts. Most companies choose to create their own NGO or advocacy group rather than contribute to an already existing organization. The Russian government remains the most powerful stakeholder in the development of certain companies' CSR agendas, resulting in the expectation that these companies support local health, educational and social welfare systems as specified by the government.

The Federal Service for Financial Markets established a corporate governance code in 2002 and has endorsed an OECD White Paper on ways to improve practices in Russia. International business associations such as the American Chamber of Commerce in Russia, the U.S.-Russia Business Council, the Association of European Businesses in Russia, and the International Business Leaders Forum, as well as Russian business associations, stress corporate governance as an important priority for their members and for Russian businesses overall. One association, the Russian Union of Industrialists and Entrepreneurs, developed a Social Charter of Russian Business in 2004 that over 200 Russian companies and organizations have since joined.

Political Violence

The large-scale public protests seen after the March 2012 Presidential elections died down towards the close of the year but were revived on January 12, 2013 when tens of thousands of people turned out to protest the Dima Yakovlev Law, which bans the adoption of Russian children by American citizens. The law was in direct retaliation to the U.S. 2012 Magnitsky Act which bans the travel of Russian human rights violators to the United States. The arrest and subsequent imprisonment of three (one has since been released) members of the Russian punk rock group "Pussy Riot" became another flashpoint for opponents of the Putin administration and raised questions regarding the state of Russia's democracy. Opposition figures have faced increasing harassment by the Russian authorities though permits for protest marches are generally approved and have, so far, avoided large scale violence.

Aleksey Navalny, anticorruption whistleblower and member of the opposition Coordination Council, was charged with three criminal cases in 2012, including prior 2009 charges for conspiring to steal timber that were resurrected following Navalny's public criticism of Investigative Committee chief Aleksandr Bastrykin. Other opposition figures, including politician Boris Nemtsov and chess professional Garry Kasparov, were detained at various points in 2012 on a variety of grounds. The resurgence of the protest movement suggests that Russians have become more politically engaged and that mass civic action will continue to be a feature of the Russian political landscape. Although the use of strong-arm tactics is not unknown in Russian commercial disputes, the U.S. Embassy is not aware of cases where foreign investments have been attacked or damaged for purely political reasons. Russia continues to struggle with an ongoing insurgency in Chechnya,

Ingushetiya and Dagestan. These republics and neighboring regions in the northern Caucasus have a high risk of violence and kidnapping.

Corruption

The Russian government stepped up its campaign against corruption in 2012. In March then-Russian President Medvedev adopted the National Anti-Corruption Plan for 2012–2013. The plan contains guidance and recommendations for the government, federal executive bodies and other government agencies on counteracting corruption, including the establishment of a legal framework for lobbying and increasing the transparency of state officials' personal finances and acceptance of gifts. In 2012, Russia adopted a law requiring individuals holding public office, state officials, municipal officials and employees of state organizations to submit information on the funds spent by them and members of their families (spouses and underage children) to acquire certain types of property, including real estate, securities, stock and vehicles. The law also requires public servants to disclose the source of the funds to confirm the legality of the acquisitions. In addition, the State Duma approved in its first reading a draft law requiring state officials, deputies, senators and governors to disclose information on their foreign bank accounts and transactions related to acquisition of property and stocks abroad. The law is expected to be adopted in 2013. Speaking at the Russian General Prosecutor's Office on the occasion of the 291st anniversary of its establishment, Sergei Ivanov, Chief of the Presidential Administration, mentioned that in 2012 over 7,000 persons charged with corruption received prison sentences and a greater number of corruption cases were initiated. One high level case led to the firing of Defense Minister Anatoly Serdyukov, although no formal charges have been announced.

Russia is a signatory to the UN Convention against Corruption, the Council of Europe's Criminal Law Convention on Corruption, and, as of 2012, the OECD Anti-Bribery Convention. The Convention criminalizes commercial bribery and prohibits both offering bribes to foreign government officials and accepting such bribes. It provides no exceptions for "grease payments," and includes foreign entities doing business in Russia, meaning these entities could be subject to liability under their own country's law, as well as Russia's. The law also increased the penalties that may be imposed upon an individual or entity found in violation. Fines and ranges of incarceration vary under the new law depending upon the type of bribe and the official involved, and the court may prevent the offender from holding certain governmental or corporate positions in the future.

However, concerns remain regarding the implementation and enforcement of the many measures required by these conventions. In recent years, there appears to be a greater number of prosecutions and convictions of mid-level bureaucrats for corruption, but real numbers are difficult to obtain and high-ranking officials are rarely prosecuted. It is important for U.S. companies, irrespective of size, to assess the business climate in the relevant market in which they will be operating or investing, and to have an effective compliance programs or measures to prevent and detect corruption, including foreign bribery. U.S. individuals and firms operating or investing in Russia should take the time to become familiar with the relevant anticorruption laws of both Russia and the United States in order to properly comply with them, and where appropriate, they should seek the advice of legal counsel.

Additional country information related to corruption can be found in the U.S. State Department's annual Human Rights Report available at http://www.state.gov/g/drl/rls/hrrpt/.

Assistance for U.S. Businesses: The U.S. Department of Commerce offers several services to aid U.S. businesses seeking to address business-related corruption issues. For example, the U.S. Commercial Service can provide services that may assist U.S. companies in conducting their due diligence as part of a company's overarching compliance program when choosing business partners or agents overseas. The U.S. Commercial Service can be reached directly through its offices in major U.S. and foreign cities, or through its Website at: www.trade.gov/cs.

The Departments of Commerce and State provide worldwide support for qualified U.S. companies bidding on foreign government contracts through the Commerce Department's Advocacy Center and State's Office of Commercial and Business Affairs. Problems, including alleged corruption by foreign governments or competitors, encountered by U.S. companies in seeking such foreign business opportunities can be brought to the attention of appropriate U.S. government officials, including local embassy personnel and through the Department of Commerce Trade Compliance Center "Report A Trade Barrier" Website at: tcc.export.gov/Report_a_Barrier/index.asp.

The U.S. Government seeks to level the global playing field for U.S. businesses by encouraging other countries to take steps to criminalize their own companies' acts of corruption, including bribery of foreign public officials, by requiring them to uphold their obligations under relevant international conventions. A U.S. firm that believes a competitor is seeking to use bribery of a foreign public official to secure a contract should bring this to the attention of appropriate U.S. agencies, as noted below.

U.S. Foreign Corrupt Practices Act (FCPA): In 1977, the United States enacted the FCPA, which makes it unlawful for a U.S. person, and certain foreign issuers of securities, to make a corrupt payment to foreign public officials for the purpose of obtaining or retaining business for or with, or directing business to, any person. The FCPA also applies to foreign firms and persons who take any act in furtherance of such a corrupt payment while in the United States. For more detailed information on the FCPA, see the FCPA Lay-Person's Guide at: www.justice.gov/criminal/fraud/fcpa/docs/lay-persons-guide.pdf.

The Department of Justice (DOJ) FCPA Opinion Procedure enables U.S. firms and individuals to request a statement of DOJ's present enforcement intentions under the anti-bribery provisions of the FCPA regarding any proposed business conduct. The details of the opinion procedure are available on DOJ's Fraud Section Website at: www.justice.gov/criminal/fraud/fcpa.

Although the Department of Commerce has no enforcement role with respect to the FCPA, it supplies general guidance to U.S. exporters who have questions about the FCPA and about international developments concerning the FCPA. For further information, see the Office of the Chief Counsel for International Counsel's website, at: http://www.ogc.doc.gov/ trans_anti_bribery.html.

Other Instruments: It is U.S. Government policy to promote good governance, including host country implementation and enforcement of anti-corruption laws and policies pursuant to their obligations under international agreements. Since enactment of the FCPA, the United States has been instrumental to the expansion of the international framework to fight corruption. Several significant components of this framework are the OECD Convention on Combating Bribery of Foreign Public Officials in International Business Transactions (OECD Anti-Bribery Convention), the United Nations Convention against Corruption (UN Convention), the Inter-American Convention against Corruption (OAS Convention), the Council of Europe Criminal and Civil Law Conventions, and a growing list of U.S. free trade agreements.

OECD Anti-Bribery Convention: The OECD Anti-Bribery Convention entered into force in February 1999. There are 38 parties to the Convention including the United States (see http://www.oecd.org/dataoecd/ 59/13/ 40272933.pdf). The Convention obligates the Parties to criminalize bribery of foreign public officials in the conduct of international business. The United

States meets its international obligations under the OECD Anti-Bribery Convention through the FCPA. In 2011, Russia passed anti-corruption legislation that clearly criminalized foreign bribery and is expected to formally accede to the Anti-Bribery Convention in early 2012.

Local Laws: U.S. firms should familiarize themselves with local anticorruption laws, and, where appropriate, seek legal counsel. While the U.S. Department of Commerce cannot provide legal advice on local laws, the Department's U.S. Commercial Service can provide assistance with navigating the host country's legal system and obtaining a list of local legal counsel.

Transparency International (TI) publishes an annual Corruption Perceptions Index (CPI). The CPI measures the perceived level of public-sector corruption in 183 countries and territories around the world. The CPI is available at: http://cpi.transparency.org/cpi2011/. TI also publishes an annual Global Corruption Report which provides a systematic evaluation of the state of corruption around the world. It includes an in-depth analysis of a focal theme, a series of country reports that document major corruption related events and developments from all continents and an overview of the latest research findings on anti-corruption diagnostics and tools. See http://www.transparency.org/publications/gcr. Transparency International-Russia also posts corruption-related research materials and findings on the following sites, all specific to Russia: www.transparency.org.ru/ INTER/index.asp and www.askjournal.ru.

The World Bank Institute publishes Worldwide Governance Indicators (WGI). These indicators assess six dimensions of governance in 213 economies, including Voice and Accountability, Political Stability and Absence of Violence, Government Effectiveness, Regulatory Quality, Rule of Law and Control of Corruption. See http://info.worldbank.org/governance/wgi/sc_country.asp. World Bank Business Environment and Enterprise Performance Surveys may also be of interest.

The World Economic Forum publishes the Global Enabling Trade Report, which presents the rankings of the Enabling Trade Index, and includes an assessment of the transparency of border administration (focused on bribe payments and corruption) and a separate segment on corruption and the regulatory environment. See http://www.weforum.org/reports/global-enabling-trade-report-2012

Global Integrity, a nonprofit organization, publishes its annual Global Integrity Report, which provides indicators with respect to governance and anti-corruption. The report highlights the strengths and weaknesses of national level anti-corruption systems. The report is available at: http://www. globalintegrity.org/ report.

Bilateral Investment Agreements

While the United States and Russia signed a bilateral investment treaty (BIT) in 1992, it is not in force due to lack of ratification by the Duma. Both countries have recently held exploratory talks regarding the feasibility of pursuing a BIT in the future. Russia shares BITs with 75 countries, 54 of which are currently in force.

The United States and Russia have shared an income tax treaty since 1992, which is designed to address the issue of double taxation and fiscal evasion with respect to taxes on income and capital. Full text of the treaty: http://www.irs.gov/pub/irs-trty/russia.pdf. There is some concern that taxation requirements have sometimes been used in Russia as a way to "raid" or illegally take possession of foreign companies, particularly small and medium enterprises.

OPIC and Other Investment Insurance Programs

The U.S. Overseas Private Investment Corporation (OPIC) has been authorized since 1992 to provide loans, loan guarantees ("financing"), and investment insurance against political risks to U.S. companies investing in Russia. OPIC's political risk insurance and financing help U.S. companies of all sizes invest in Russia. OPIC insures against three political risks: expropriation; political violence; and currency inconvertibility. OPIC recently announced that political risk insurance now covers private equity fund investments. To meet the demands of larger projects in Russia and worldwide, OPIC can insure up to USD 250 million per project and up to USD 300 million for projects in the oil and gas sector with offshore, hard currency revenues. Projects in the oil and gas sector with offshore, hard currency revenues may be approved for an exposure limit up to USD 400 million if the project receives a credit evaluation ("shadow rating") of investment grade or higher. The individual per project exposure limit for financing is USD 250 million. The maximum combined (insurance and financing) exposure limit to OPIC on a single project is USD 400 million. OPIC has no minimum investment size requirements. OPIC also makes equity capital available for investments in Russia by guaranteeing long-term loans to private equity investment funds. Detailed information about OPIC's programs can be accessed at www.opic.gov. Russia is also a member of the World Bank's Multilateral Investment Guarantee Agency.

Labor

The Russian labor market remains fragmented, characterized by limited labor mobility across regions and consequent wage and employment differentials. Earnings inequalities are substantial, enforcement of labor standards is relatively weak, and collective bargaining is underdeveloped. Employers regularly complain about shortages of qualified labor. This is due in part to weak linkages between the education system and the labor market. In addition, the economy suffers from a general shortage of highly skilled labor. Businesses face increasing labor costs as competition over a limited pool of workers intensifies. On the other hand, a large number of inefficient SOEs with high vacancy rates offer workers unattractive, uncompetitive salaries and benefits.

The 2002 Labor Code governs labor standards in Russia. The enforcement of worker safety rules continues to be a major issue, as enterprises are often unable or unwilling to invest in safer equipment or to enforce safety standards.

The rate of actual unemployment (calculated according to ILO methodology) in 2012 remained relatively low, and declined from 6.6% in January 2012 to historic low of 5.2% in August and September. Average unemployment in urban districts (4.4% as of November) is much lower than in rural districts (8.3%). Two regions in the North Caucasus have the highest unemployment rates in the country: Ingushetia (47% as of September-November) and Chechnya (30.8%). In stark contrast, the unemployment rate is only 0.6% in Moscow and 1.1% in St. Petersburg.

Official statistics registered only five labor strikes in January-November 2012. Independent commentators, however, noted 258 protests during January-November 2012, including 87 that involved the complete or partial cessation of work. The majority of labor disputes occurred in the manufacturing sector.

The primary causes of labor disputes were wage arrears, company reorganization or closure, low pay, and layoffs. Approximately 45% of Russia's workforce is unionized. The government generally adheres to ILO conventions protecting worker rights but often fails to enforce them.

Foreign Trade Zones/Free Ports

Russia has 26 Special Economic Zones (SEZs), which fall in one of four categories: industrial and production zones; technology and innovation zones; tourist and recreation zones; and port zones. Enterprises operating within SEZs enjoy a range of benefits that the Ministry of Economic Development (MED) – which manages the SEZ program – estimates can save investors up to 30% of the cost of doing business. Specifically, investors enjoy streamlined administrative requirements and procedures, a more favorable customs regime (including the waiver of import duties and refunds of the value-added-tax), and reduced tax rates on income, property, land, and transport. SEZ investors also receive discounts on infrastructure expenses, including facilities and utilities costs. Such benefits are extended for an agreed introductory period, often lasting five years.

In a Federation Council meeting in December 2012 there was wide support for a proposal to leverage the SEZs in attracting new foreign direct investment rather than working to place companies that have already decided to invest in Russia within an SEZ. How the MED will go about refocusing the SEZ mission to attract investment is unclear; but the proposal reflects broad interest in improving the performance of the existing SEZs, which have met with mixed results to date.

Lack of interest from foreign investors in addition to environmental concerns led to the closure of the proposed Kaliningrad tourist and recreational zone SEZ in late 2012. The majority of SEZ investments are still listed as "planned," meaning investors are still able to back out of commitments. The Russian government has been hesitant to go forward with major SEZ infrastructure projects.

Detailed information about the benefits and results of Russia's SEZs can be found at the MED's SEZ website:_http://www.economy.gov.ru/minec/activity/sections/sez/main/.

Independent of the SEZs, in 2010 President Medvedev launched an initiative to establish the Skolkovo Innovation Center in the Moscow suburbs to promote investment in high-technology startup businesses, research, and commercialization of technological innovation. Inspired by the model of Silicon Valley, Skolkovo "resident companies" can receive a broad range of benefits, including complete exemption from profit tax, value-added tax, property taxes, and import duties, and partial exemption from social fund payments. Applicants for residency are evaluated and selected by an international admission board; company performance is monitored to ensure continued qualification for benefits. According to the Skolkovo Foundation, over 200 companies have been selected as residents thus far.

Foreign Direct Investment Statistics

Table 1 shows flows of foreign investment into Russia by country for the first nine months of 2012, compared to the same period in 2011. Total foreign investment decreased by 14% year-on-year.

According to Russian statistical practice, total foreign investment numbers include direct investment (FDI), portfolio investment, and other investment (largely trade credits).

FDI flows into Russia, however, increased slightly in 2012, rising by 4 %; the largest share came from Switzerland. FDI from the Netherlands and Cyprus is consistently high, reflecting the fact that most FDI coming from these countries is either returning or reinvested Russian capital through subsidiaries or off-shore "shell" vehicles. (Note: The data in the tables below are from the Russian State Statistical Service (RosStat) and differ from data maintained by the Central Bank of Russia and the U.S. Department of Commerce.)

Table 1. Top Investors - By Year (in USD million)

Country	Jan-Sep 2012		Jan-Sep 2011		Jan-Sep 2010	
	Total	FDI	Total	FDI	Total	FDI
Switzerland	43,252	88	69,115	70.1	3,398	64.5
Netherlands	15,676	909	13,218	3,023	7,507	943
Cyprus	11,788	3,842	12,972	2,758	5,635	1,912
Germany	3,799	1,119	8,169	1,480	7,520	1,095
UK	10,618	500	6,336	176	4,240	430
All Others	29,330	5,819	23,976	4,228	19,189	3,751
Total	114,463	12,277	133,784	11,736	47,488	8,196

The numbers in Table 2 represent the accumulated stock of total foreign investment in Russia by originating country, including FDI, portfolio, and "other" investment as of September 30, 2012, compared to the amount accumulated a year prior. Source: RosStat.

Table 2. Top Investors - Accumulated Basis (in USD million)

Country	As of Sep 30, 2012		As of Sep 30, 2011		As of Sep 30, 2010	
	Total	FDI	Total	FDI	Total	FDI
Cyprus	78,566	53,357	69,057	47,290	57,600	40,377
Netherlands	59,223	21,723	46,295	23,328	44,184	22,790
Luxembourg	39,808	1,191	35,051	643	32,228	652
Germany	24,757	11,393	29,779	11,386	22,656	8,332
China	27,792	1,346	27,356	1,238	10,543	931
All Others	123,198	46,298	115,650	42,529	98,743	37,074
Total	353,344	135,308	323,178	126,415	265,954	110,156

Table 3 shows total foreign investment by region over the first nine months of 2011, compared to the same period in 2010. RosStat has not provided updated data on regional foreign investment for 2012. In the 2010-2011 comparison, Moscow continued to attract the largest volume of investments (63.4% of total foreign investment), mainly due to the concentration of companies' headquarters and consumers with high purchasing power. Source: RosStat. (Note: includes direct, portfolio and "other" investment.)

Table 3. Foreign Investment – Top Regions (in USD million)

	Jan-Sep 2011			Jan-Sep 2010		
	Amount	%	Rank	Amount	%	Rank
Moscow (city)	84,878	63.4%	1	15,816	33.3%	1
Tyumen Region	9,821	7.3%	2	701	1.5%	11
Sakhalin Region	6,570	4.9%	3	3,611	7.6%	4
St. Petersburg	3,972	3.0%	4	3,723	7.8%	3
Belgorod Region	3,171	2.4%	5	24.7	0.1%	58
Others	25,371	19.0%		23,612	49.7%	
Total	133,784	100%		47,488	100.0%	

Table 4 shows investment by sector over the first nine months of 2012, compared to the same period in 2011. Total investment decreased in five of the ten top sectors. Foreign investment into the financial sector dropped off precipitously, with a decrease of 42%. Given the continued weakness of the global economy, investors are reducing their exposure to emerging markets, including Russia. Foreign, particularly European, banks are also repatriating profits from their Russian subsidiaries. Source: RosStat.

Table 4. Foreign Investment: Top Sectors (in USD million)

Industry/Sector	Jan-Sep 2012		Jan-Sep 2011		Jan-Sep 2010	
	%	Amount	%	Amount	%	Amount
Finance	33.46%	38,300	49.10%	65,711	3.70%	1,764
Extraction of Fuel	10.60%	12,136	9.60%	12,850	17.10%	8,115
Wholesale and Retail Trade	15.79%	18,074	9.20%	12,363	18.30%	8,688
Production of coke and oil products	10.78%	12,338	7.50%	9,997	10.50%	4,980
Metallurgy	6.05%	6,927	4.40%	5,902	10.40%	4,950
Transport and Communications	2.95%	3,377	4.10%	5,494	8.30%	3,952
Real Estate and Related Services	6.25%	7,150	3.60%	4,782	8.10%	3,843
Chemical Industry	2.09%	2,387	2.70%	3,636	3.50%	1,679
Food Industry	1.38%	1,583	1.50%	1,964	3.90%	1,866
Production of vehicles	2.45%	2,802	1.40%	1,845	3.30%	1,569
All Others	9.20%	9,389	6.90%	9,240	12.80%	6,082
Total	100.00%	114,463	100.00%	133,784	100.00%	47,488

Table 5 shows stocks of Russian FDI abroad as of September 30, 2012 and September 30, 2011, as well as flows of Russian FDI abroad for the first nine months of 2012, compared to the same period in 2011. Russian FDI stocks abroad increased in five of seven top destinations for FDI (data from 2011 was unavailable for Luxembourg and the United Kingdom). Source: RosStat.

Table 5. Top Destinations of Russian FDI - By Year (in USD million)

Country	as of Sep 30, 2012		as of Sep 30, 2011	
	Stock	Flow	Stock	Flow
Netherlands	31,049	6,848	25,067	8,427

Table 5. (Continued)

Country	as of Sep 30, 2012		as of Sep 30, 2011	
	Stock	Flow	Stock	Flow
Cyprus	25,686	10,834	14,280	842
Switzerland	8,115	38,641	2,814	328
United States	7,880	642	6,663	439
United Kingdom	6,270	7,528	N/A	N/A
Luxembourg	6,206	213	N/A	N/A
Belarus	5,820	5,877	2,685	629

In: Brazil, Russia, India, China, and South Africa   ISBN: 978-1-62618-627-9
Editor: Sandra C. Owens   © 2013 Nova Science Publishers, Inc.

Chapter 3

2013 INVESTMENT CLIMATE STATEMENT: INDIA*

Bureau of Economic and Business Affairs

OPENNESS TO, AND RESTRICTIONS UPON, FOREIGN INVESTMENT

India's sizeable and rapidly growing domestic market, well-regulated and growing financial markets, large English-speaking population, and its stable democratic government make it an attractive place for investors. However, India underperforms its vast potential.

Major areas of concern include rampant corruption, complex and lengthy investment and business approval processes, antiquated land acquisition and labor laws, and poor contract enforcement.

India's historical preference for economic self-sufficiency informs current and proposed industrial and trade policies that protect domestic manufacturing, agriculture, and other sectors. In 2012, the World Bank's International Finance Corporation ranks India 132 among 183 world economies in its ease of doing business survey and the Organization for Economic Co-operation and Development ranks India high as a closed economy in its Foreign Direct Investment Restrictiveness Index.

---

* This is an edited, reformatted and augmented version of Bureau of Economic and Business Affairs, dated February 2013.

Furthermore, India's GDP growth slow-down in the past year, its large fiscal and current account deficits, and persistent inflation raise concerns about its economic outlook. In recent months, the government has taken some steps to ease Foreign Direct Investment (FDI) restrictions in certain sectors and to improve corporate governance laws.

However, further policy reforms have been hung up in a stalemated parliament giving rise to uncertainty about the pace and efficacy of additional measures for improving the investment climate.

Power and decision-making is decentralized in India, therefore investors should be prepared to face varying business and economic conditions across India's 28 states and 7 union territories. There are differences at the state-level in political leadership, quality of governance, regulations, taxation, labor relations, and education levels.

Although India prides itself on its rule of law, its courts have cases backlogged for years. By some accounts more than 30 million cases could be pending in various courts, including India's high courts.

Nevertheless, companies have found ways to succeed in this difficult market. Indian conglomerates and high technology companies are by many measures equal in sophistication and prominence to their international counterparts.

Certain industrial sectors, such as information technology, telecommunications, and engineering are globally recognized for their innovation and competitiveness. Foreign companies operating in India highlight that success requires a long-term planning horizon and a state-by-state strategy to adapt to the complexity and diversity of India's markets.

Business Environment Indices:

- Transparency International Corruption Index (TI): India's ranking remained in the lower third tier of countries. http://cpi.transparency.org/cpi2012/results/#myAnchor1

- Heritage Economic Freedom: The marginal change in India's score reflects some improvements in labor freedom that were offset by declining scores in business freedom, freedom from corruption, government spending, and monetary freedom. http://www.heritage.org/index/country/india

- World Bank/IFC "Doing Business 2013:" India's overall ranking has remained fairly consistent over the last four years. India's ranking has worsened in the areas of 'starting a business' (173rd), 'dealing with construction permits' (182nd), 'protecting investors' (49th), 'trading across borders' (127th), 'enforcing contracts' (184th) and 'paying taxes' (152nd). India ranked as the world's sixth slowest country in terms of the number of days it takes to resolve a commercial investment dispute. (http://www.doingbusiness.org/~/media/GIAWB /Doing%20Business/Documents/Annual-Reports/English/DB13-full-report.pdf

- Legatum Index: This global study of the factors that drive and restrain national prosperity, reflects a consistent decline in India's ranking since 2009. India's failure to maintain and improve healthcare (104th), education and literacy rates (100th), safety and security (114th), and social capital (138th) are a few examples that explain the country's decline in the rankings.

Measure	Year	Index/Ranking
TI Corruption Index	2012	94/176
Heritage Economic Freedom	2012	123/170
World Bank Doing Business	2013	132/185
Legatum Index	2012	110/142
MCC Gov't Effectiveness	2013	98%
MCC Rule of Law	2013	98%
MCC Control of Corruption	2013	73%
MCC Fiscal Policy	2013	4%
MCC Trade Policy	2013	35%
MCC Regulatory Quality	2013	84%
MCC Business Start Up	2013	47%
MCC Land Rights Access	2013	61%
MCC Natural Resource Mgmt	2013	35%

There are two channels for foreign investment: the "automatic route" and the "government route." Investments entering via the "automatic route," are not required to seek an overall approval from the central government. The investor is expected to notify the Reserve Bank of India (RBI) of its investment using the FC form within 30 days of inward receipts and the issuance of shares (www.rbi.org.in/scripts).

The title "automatic route" is somewhat of a misnomer in that investments in most sectors will still require some interaction with the Indian government at the state, or national levels or both.

Investments requiring government approval, also known as the "government route," are subject to seeking required authorization from the principal ministry and/or from the Foreign Investment Promotion Board (FIPB). The rules regulating government approval for investments vary from industry to industry and the approving government entity varies depending on the applicant and the product.

For example the Ministry of Commerce and Industry (MOCI) Department of Industrial Policy and Promotion (DIPP) oversees single-brand product retailing investment proposals, as well as proposals made by Non-Resident Indians (NRIs), and Overseas Corporate Bodies (OCBs).

An OCB is a company, partnership firm, or other corporate entity that is at least 60% owned, directly or indirectly, by NRIs, including overseas trusts. MOCI's Department of Commerce approves investment proposals from export-oriented units (i.e., industrial companies that intend to export their entire production of goods and services from India abroad).

The jointly-led Ministry of Finance and MOCI Foreign Investment Promotion Board approves most other investment applications.

All new investments require a number of industrial approvals and clearances from different authorities such as Pollution Control Board, Chief Inspector of Factories, Electricity Board, and Municipal Corporation (locally elected entities), among others.

To fast track the approval process for investments greater than USD 200 million, the Government of India in December 2012 established the Cabinet Committee on Investment (CCI). CCI is led by the Prime Minister and is expected to fast track large new investment proposals.

Sector-Specific Guidelines for FDI in key industries

- Banking: Aggregate foreign investment from all sources in all private banks is capped at 74%. For state-owned banks, the foreign ownership limit is 20%. According to the 2011 road map for foreign bank entry, there are three distinct ways to enter the Indian banking sector. The first is by establishing a branch in India. The second is to establish a wholly owned subsidiary, although it is important to note that foreign banks are permitted to have either branches or subsidiaries, but not both. The third is to establish a subsidiary with total foreign investment of up to 74%. Foreign investors are also allowed to acquire an ailing bank.

  Although the RBI has never authorized this type of transaction, FII is limited to 10% of the total paid-up capital and 5% in cases where the investment is from a foreign bank/bank group. Voting rights in private banks and state-owned banks are currently capped at 10% and 1%, respectively, and are not considered ownership. The Banking Regulation (Amendment) Bill, which would align voting rights in private banks with shareholding, remains in a Parliamentary committee and has yet to be introduced.

- Manufacturing: 100% FDI is allowed in most sub-categories of the manufacturing sector. However, the government maintains set asides for MSEs (Micro and Small Enterprises). The Government of India definition for 'MSE' is a company with less than USD 1 million in plant and machinery.

Any investment in manufacturing that would not qualify as an MSE and manufactures items reserved for the MSE sector must enter via the Government route for FDI greater than 24%. Since 1997, the government has steadily decreased the number of sectors it protects under the national small-scale industry (SSI) policy. At its peak in the late 1990s, more than 800 categories were protected. The list is publicly available here: http://www.dcmsme.gov.in/publications /reserveditems/reserved2010.pdf.

The 2011 National Manufacturing Policy (NMP) provides the framework for India's local manufacturing requirements in various sectors including in the Information and Communications Technology (ICT) and clean energy sectors.

- Non-Banking Financial Companies (NBFC): 100% FDI is allowed via the automatic route. NBFCs include: merchant banking, underwriting, portfolio management, financial consulting, stock-brokerage, asset management, venture capital, credit rating agencies, housing finance, leasing and finance, credit card businesses, foreign exchange brokerages, money changers, factoring and custodial services, investment advisory services, and micro and rural credit.

All investments are subject to the following minimum capitalization norms: USD 500,000 upfront for investments with up to 51% foreign ownership; USD 5 million upfront for investments with 51% to 74.9% ownership; USD 50 million total, with USD 7.5 million required up-front and the remaining balance within 24 months, for investments with more than 75% ownership. 100% foreign-owned NBFCs, with a minimum capitalization of USD 50 million, are allowed to set up unlimited numbers of subsidiaries for specific NBFC activities and are not required to bring in additional capital.

Sector	% FDI	Route	Note
Advertising and Film	100%	Automatic	Includes film production, exhibition, distribution, and related services and products
Agriculture (Farming)	None		
Agriculture-related Activities	100%	Automatic	Seed industry, floriculture, horticulture, animal husbandry, aquaculture, fish farming, and cultivation of vegetables and mushrooms
	100%	Government	Tea plantations. Five years after making the initial investment in a tea plantation, foreign investors are required divest ownership to allow for at least 26% Indian ownership.
Airline Carriers (air transport services)	49%	Government	Scheduled and non-scheduled airline carriers also (NRIs may own 100% of a domestic airline.) The decision was announced in September, 2012, by the Cabinet Committee on Economic Affairs. Investments are required to follow relevant SEBI regulations that include the Issue of Capital and Disclosure Requirements (ICDR) Regulations and the Substantial Acquisition of Shares and Takeovers (SAST) Regulations. (http://pib.nic.in/newsite/PrintRelease.aspx?relid=87785)
	74%	Automatic	Non-scheduled, chartered, and/or cargo airlines.
	100%	Automatic	Investments in helicopter and seaplane services. Investors are required to seek approval from the Directorate General of Civil Aviation.
Airport Infrastructure	100%	Automatic	Green-field projects
	74%	Automatic	Existing projects. FDI greater than 74% requires FIPB approval
	49%	Automatic	Ground-handling businesses at airports. (NRIs are allowed 100%).
	49-74%	Government	
	100%	Automatic	Maintenance and repair operations, flight training institutes, and technical training institutes.
Alcoholic Distillation and Brewing	100%	Automatic	Requires a license from DIPP under the provisions of the Industries (Development and Regulation) Act, 1951.
Asset Reconstruction Companies	49%	Government	(FII is not allowed)Where any individual investment exceeds 10% of the equity, investors are required to seek approval as delineated in the Securitization and Reconstruction of Financial Assets and Enforcement of Security Interest (SARFAESI) Act, 2002.
Automobiles	100%	Automatic	Local content requirements and/or export obligations apply.

Sector	% FDI	Route	Note
Broadcasting	26%	Government	(FDI, NRI, persons of Indian origin, and portfolio investment) frequency modulation terrestrial broadcasting. Subject to guidelines issued by the Ministry of Information and Broadcasting
	49%	Automatic	Direct-to-home broadcasting and mobile TV. TV channels, irrespective of ownership or management control, have to up-link from India and comply with the broadcast code issued by the Ministry of Information and Broadcasting.
	74%	Government	
	26%	Government	News and current affairs channels with up-linking from India, including portfolio investment
	100%	Government	Entertainment and general interest channels
	49%	Government	Establishing up-linking hub/teleports (http://pib.nic.in/newsite/PrintRelease.aspx?relid=87787)
Business Services	100%	Automatic	Data processing, software development, and computer consultancy services. One hundred% FDI is allowed for call centers and business processing outsourcing (BPO) organizations, subject to certain conditions.
Cable Network	49%		Approval is required, as articulated in the Cable Television Networks Rules, 1994
Coal/Lignite	100%		Setting up or operating power projects and coal mines for captive consumption.
	100%	Automatic	Coal processing plants, so long as the equity recipient does not sell processed coal in the open market.
	100	Automatic	Mining of coal or lignite for captive consumption
Coffee and Rubber Processing and Warehousing	100%	Automatic	
Commodity Exchanges	23% (FII) 26% (FDI)	Government	FII purchases shall be restricted to secondary markets only and no single foreign investor/entity can hold more than 5% of the total paid-up capital. (www.dipp.nic.in/English/Policies/FDI_)
Construction Development Projects	100%	Automatic	Permitted in the construction and maintenance of roads, highways, vehicular bridges, tunnels, ports and harbors, townships, housing, commercial buildings, resorts, educational institutions, and infrastructure. (Non-resident Indians are not authorized to own land.) Subject to certain minimum capitalization and minimum area-of-development requirements. Since 2010, the minimum capitalization requirement has been USD 10 million for wholly owned subsidiaries and USD 5 million for joint ventures with Indian partners.

Sector	% FDI	Route	Note
			In the case of serviced housing plots, a minimum of 10 hectares (25 acres) must be developed, while in the case of construction-development projects, the minimum built-up area must be 50,000 square meters (approx. 538,000 square feet). At least 50% of the project must be developed within five years from the date of obtaining all statutory clearances.
Credit Information Companies	49% (FDI) 24% (FII)	Government	Requires FIPB and RBI approval No single investor/entity can own shares worth more than 10% of the total paid-up capital. Furthermore, any acquisition in excess of 1% requires mandatory reporting to RBI.
Courier Services (Other Than Distribution of Letters)	100%	Government	
Defense and Strategic Industries	26%		Subject to a DIPP license in consultation with the Defense Ministry. Production of arms and ammunition is subject to additional FDI guidelines. Purchase and price preferences may be given to Public Sector Enterprises as per Department of Public Enterprise guidelines. The licensee must establish adequate safety and security procedures once the authorization is granted and production begins.
Drug/Pharmaceuticals	100% 100%	Automatic Government	Greenfield investments Brown-field investments
E-commerce	100%		Business-to-business e-commerce under the government approval route. No FDI is allowed in retail e-commerce.
Education Services	100%	Automatic	In practical terms restrictions limit investments to education service providers rather than educational institutions. The Foreign Educational Institutions (Regulation of Entry and Operations, Maintenance of Quality and Prevention of Commercialization) Bill pending in Parliament would, if passed, allow foreign universities to establish campuses independently without working with an Indian partner institution, but with conditions attached.
Food Processing	100%	Automatic	For fruit and vegetable processing, dairy products, meat and poultry products, fishing and fish processing, grains, confections, consumer and convenience foods, soft bottling, food parks, cold chain, and warehousing. The exception is for alcoholic beverages and beer, where a license is required.

Sector	% FDI	Route	Note
	100%	Automatic	For cold storage facilities.
Hazardous chemicals	100%	Automatic	A DIPP license is required under the provisions of the Industries (Development and Regulation) Act, 1951.
Health Services	100%	Automatic	
Hotels, Tourism, and Restaurants	100%	Automatic	
Housing/Real Estate	None		NRIs who obtain "Overseas Citizenship of India" status are allowed to own property and invest in India as if they were citizens. NRIs may invest up to 100% FDI with prior government approval in the real estate sector and in integrated townships including housing, commercial premises, resorts, and hotels, as well as in projects such as the manufacture of building materials.
Industrial explosives	100%	Automatic	Manufacturers of explosives or materials deemed by the Indian authorities as explosives are required to obtain a license to set up factory operations from the state government's industry commissioner.
Industrial Parks	100%	Automatic	The industrial park must include at least ten units with no single unit occupying more than 50% of the area, and at least 66% of the area is made available for industrial activity.
Information Technology	100%	Automatic	For software and electronics development. However no FDI is allowed in companies that develop software for the aerospace and defense sectors.
Insurance	26%	Automatic	Investors must obtain a license from the Insurance Regulatory and Development Authority (IRDA). In October 2012, the Cabinet cleared an amendment to raise the cap on foreign investment to 49%. The bill is pending in the Parliament.
Infrastructure Companies in the Securities Market (i.e., stock exchanges, depositories, and clearing corporations)	26%	Government	Over and above the FDI limit, FII's are allowed to buy shares through the secondary markets up to 23% of the paid up capital through the automatic route. FIIs are only allowed to invest via secondary markets.
Legal services	None		In March 2010, a Chennai-based attorney, on behalf of the Association of Indian Lawyers, filed a writ of petition in the Madras High Court against 31 foreign law firms, the Bar Council of India, and the Ministry of External Affairs in order to prevent foreign law firms from practicing in India. The Madras High Court has repeatedly delayed a decision in order to give the court more time to consult with foreign firms.

Sector	% FDI	Route	Note
			The outcome of the case remains unresolved and the future of foreign law firms practicing in India remains uncertain. The petitioner in the Madras case and other opponents to allowing foreign investment in legal services, with a particular focus on U.S. attorneys, insist foreign firms should be barred from practicing law in India until there is reciprocity in the U.S. market. Law firms from the UK and other countries have found alternatives to the ban on FDI.
Lottery, Gambling, and Betting	None		
Mining	100%	Automatic	For diamonds and precious stones, gold/silver, and other mineral mining and exploration.
	100%	Government	For mining and mineral separation of titanium minerals and ores.
Pensions	None		The Parliament is currently considering a law that would establish India's Pension Fund Development and Regulatory Authority and lift the ban on FDI. It is unclear when the draft legislation will become law.
Petroleum	100%	Automatic (tax incentives, production sharing, and other terms and conditions apply)	Discovered small fields
			Refining with domestic private company
			Petroleum product/pipeline
			Petrol/diesel retail outlets
			LNG Pipeline
			Exploration
			Investment Financing
			Market study and formulation
	49%	Government	Refining by public sector company, disinvestment is prohibited
Pollution Control	100%	Automatic	For equipment manufacture, consulting, and management services.
Ports and harbors	100%	Automatic	For construction and manufacturing of ports and harbors. Security clearances from the Ministry of Defense are required for all bidders on port projects, and only the bids of cleared bidders will be considered.

Sector	% FDI	Route	Note
Power	100%	Automatic	For the power sector (except atomic energy) which includes generation, transmission, and distribution of electricity, and power trading. FDI up to 49% is permitted in power exchanges; such foreign investment would be subject to an FDI limit of 26% and an FII limit of 23% of the paid-up capital. For power exchanges, FII investment would be permitted under the automatic route and FDI would be permitted under the government approval route.
Print Media	26%	Government	Newspapers and news periodicals.
	100%	Government	Printing science and technology magazines/journals.
	100%	Government	Publication of facsimile editions of foreign newspapers.
Professional services	100%	Automatic	For most consulting and professional services, including accounting services.
Research and Development Services	100%	Automatic	
Railways	None		Train operations
	100%	Government	Auxiliary areas such as rail track construction, ownership of rolling stock, provisioning of container services, and container depots.
	100%	Government	Building of "fixed railway infrastructure" including railway lines for the purpose of increasing port connectivity with industrial and logistical parks, mines, and other parts of the country.
Retailing (single brand)	100%	Government	Investors are required to meet a 30% local content requirement sourced from domestic SMEs. (http://pib.nic.in/newsite/PrintRelease.aspx?relid=87766).
Retailing (multi-brand)	51%	state-by-state basis	Investment is conditioned on 1) state government opening of the retail sector 2) investment in cities with a population greater than a million residents, 3) invest a minimum of 50% in developing backend infrastructure, and 4) source 30% of the total value of the products sold from Indian SMEs.
Roads	100%	Automatic	Including Highways, and Mass Rapid Transport Systems
Satellites	74%	Government	For the establishment and operation of satellites.
Security Agencies	49%	Government	
Shipping	74%	Automatic	
Storage and Warehouse Services	100%	Automatic	Including for cold storage warehousing of agricultural products.

Sector	% FDI	Route	Note
	74%	Government	This sector is considered to be 'sensitive' by the GOI and therefore foreign investment is carefully scrutinized and monitored. FDI in the telecom services sector can be made directly or indirectly in the operating company or through a holding company, subject to licensing and security requirements.
	49%	Automatic	In telecom services such as basic, cellular, access services, national/international long distance, V-Sat, public mobile radio trunked services, global mobile, unified personal communication services, ISP gateways, radio-paging, and end-to-end services.
	74%	Government	Equipment manufacturing. Note: Some telecommunications investments require 26%
	49%	Automatic	divestment within the first five years of the investment.
	100%	Government	Internet service providers (ISP) with and without international gateways, including those for
	49%	Automatic	satellite and marine cables.
	100%		Fiber-optic, right-of-way, duct space, voice mail, and email. Note: Some telecommunications investments require 26% divestment within the first five years of the investment.
Trading/ Wholesale	100%	Automatic	For exporting, bulk imports with export warehouse sales, and cash-and-carry wholesale trading. A wholesaler/cash-and-carry trader cannot open a retail shop to sell directly to consumers.

CONVERSION AND TRANSFER POLICIES

The Indian Rupee is fully convertible for current account transactions, which are regulated under the Foreign Exchange Management Rules, 2000. Prior RBI approval is required for acquiring foreign currency above certain limits for specific purposes (e.g., foreign travel, consulting services, and foreign studies). Capital account transactions are open for foreign investors and subject to various clearances. In recent years, with growing foreign exchange reserves, the Indian government has taken additional steps to relax foreign exchange and capital account controls for Indian companies and individuals. For example, since 2007, individuals are permitted to transfer up to USD 200,000 per year abroad for any purpose without approval. On December 31, 2012, the exchange rate was Rupees 55/$, compared to Rupees 53.2/$ and 44.8/$ at the end of 2011 and 2010, respectively. The slow economic recovery in many of India's trading partners coupled with domestic inflationary pressure has contributed to the Rupee decline visa vie other hard currencies. Other conversion restrictions include:

- NRI investment in real estate may be subject to a "lock-in" period.
- Profits and dividend remittances, as current account transactions, are permitted without RBI approval but income tax payment clearance is required. There are generally no transfer delays beyond 60 days.
- RBI approval is needed to remit the proceeds of sales of assets.
- Foreign partners may sell their shares to resident Indian investors without RBI approval, provided the shares were eligible to be repatriated out of India.
- Global Depository Receipts and American Depository Receipts proceeds from abroad may be retained without restrictions except for an end-use ban on investment in real estate and stock markets. FIPB approval is required in some cases. Up to USD 1 million per year may be remitted for transfer of assets into India.
- Foreign institutional investors (FII) may transfer funds from Rupee to foreign currency accounts and vice-versa at the market exchange rate. They may also repatriate capital, capital gains, dividends, interest income, and any compensation from the sale of rights offerings, net of all taxes, without RBI approval. The RBI authorizes automatic approval to Indian industries for the payment associated with foreign collaboration agreements, royalty, and lump sum fees for transfer of

technology and payments for the use of trademark and brand names with no limits. Royalties and lump sum payments are taxed at 10%.

- Foreign banks may remit profits and surpluses to their headquarters, subject to the banks' compliance with the Banking Regulation Act, 1949. Banks are permitted to offer foreign currency-Rupee swaps without limits to enable customers to hedge their foreign currency liabilities. They may also offer forward cover to non-resident entities on FDI deployed after 1993.

EXPROPRIATION AND COMPENSATION

India's image as an investment destination was tarnished in 2010 and 2011 by high profile graft cases in the construction and telecom sectors, exacerbating existing private sector concerns about the government of India's uneven application of its policies. In October 2012, India's Supreme Court cancelled 122 telecom licenses and the authorized spectrum held by eight operators under what came to be known as the 2G scandal. Some of the operators affected by this cancellation stated in media reporting that they may exit India rather than wait for new market rules to be issued. The U.S. Government continues to urge the Government of India to foster an attractive and reliable investment climate by reducing barriers to investment and minimizing bureaucratic hurdles for businesses. India and its political subdivisions would benefit from providing a secure legal and regulatory framework for the private sector, as well as institutionalized dispute resolution mechanisms that expedite commercial disagreements.

DISPUTE SETTLEMENT

Foreign investors frequently complain about a lack of "sanctity of contracts." According to the World Bank, India continues to be the sixth slowest country in the world in terms of the total number of days it takes to resolve a dispute. Indian courts are reported to be understaffed and lacking the technology needed to resolve the current backlog of unsettled cases. Media reports estimate that India has between 30 and 40 million backlogged legal cases countrywide. Former Indian Law Minister Salman Khurshid acknowledged the need to modernize the country's antiquated legal system to support economic growth. According to a 2012 PRS Legislative survey, a local research center and think tank, India has seen an increase of pending cases by 30% over the last decade. In an attempt to align its adjudication of commercial contract disputes with the rest of the world, in 1996, India enacted the Arbitration and Conciliation Act based on the UNCITRAL (United Nations Commission on International Trade Law) model. Foreign awards are enforceable under multilateral conventions like the Geneva Convention. The Indian government established the International Center for Alternative Dispute Resolution (ICADR) as an autonomous organization under the Ministry of Law and Justice to promote the settlement of domestic and international disputes through alternate dispute resolution. The World Bank funded ICADR to conduct training for mediators in commercial disputes settlement.

India is a member of the New York Convention of 1958 on the recognition and enforcement of foreign arbitral awards. Despite having signed this agreement, the Embassy is aware of several cases in which Indian firms have filed spurious cases with Indian courts to delay paying the awards granted in arbitration to the U.S. party. India has yet to become a member of the International Center for the Settlement of Investment Disputes. The Permanent Court of Arbitration (PCA, The Hague) and the Indian Law Ministry agreed, in 2007, to establish a regional PCA office in New Delhi to provide an arbitration forum to match the facilities offered at The Hague at a far lower cost. Since then, no further progress has been made in establishing the office. In November 2009, the Department of Revenue's Central Board of Direct Taxes established eight dispute resolution panels (DRPs) across the country to settle the transfer-pricing tax disputes of domestic and foreign companies in a faster and more cost-effective manner.

PERFORMANCE REQUIREMENTS AND INCENTIVES

The government is currently pursuing local content requirements in specific areas including ICT, electronics, and clean energy to increase the manufacturing sector's contribution to GDP. Foreign investors in India express concern about these policies and the negative impact they may have on India's investment climate, especially if the GOI applies local content requirements to the private sector. The GOI has already issued finalized notifications on local content requirements for ICT equipment in government procurement. http://commerce

Companies are free to select the location of their industrial projects. Foreign investors complain that antiquated land acquisition laws and uneven zoning regulations prevent them from establishing factories in their preferred location. The Ministry of Commerce and Industry, in recognition of the trouble foreign and domestic investors experience in acquiring land, has set aside land for 14 integrated industrial townships called National Investment and Manufacturing Zones (NIMZs). NIMZs offer investors a one-stop-approval process for investment; state-of-the-art infrastructure; pre-zoned land for industrial use; and other tax benefits. Seven basic NOC's (No Objection Certificate's) are required for almost all investments and projects:

1. Tree Authority
2. Storm Water and Drain Department
3. Sewerage Department
4. Hydraulic Department
5. Environmental Department (concerned with debris management)
6. Traffic and Coordination Department
7. CFO (fire department clearance)

Visa Regulations

Foreign nationals executing projects and/or contracts in India are required to obtain an "employment" visa. All foreigners (including foreigners of Indian origin) visiting India for more than 180 days -- Student Visa, Medical Visa, Research Visa and Employment Visa -- are required to register with the Foreigners Regional Registration Officer (FRRO) in Delhi or the Foreigners Registration Officer (FRO) in their jurisdiction within 14 days of their arrival.

The employment of foreigners for periods longer than 12 months requires the approval of the Ministry of Home Affairs (MHA). Recently, MHA eased the rule requiring foreign nationals traveling to India on a multiple-entry Indian tourist visa to wait a minimum of two months between visits to India, eliminating it entirely for most travelers.

The Department of Telecommunications under the Ministry of Communications and Information Technology closely monitors the employment of foreign nationals in the telecom sector. Senior leadership and managers of the security operations, among others, are required to be citizens of India or obtain a security clearance from the Ministry of Home Affairs

(MHA). More details regarding this and related rules are available on the MHA website: http://mha.nic.in/foreigDiv/pdfs/TourVISA-Schm.pdf.

Taxes

The GOI provides a 10-year tax holiday for knowledge-based start-ups. Many states use local tax incentives to attract investment, and these benefits vary by state and by sector. Recent Government of India efforts to strengthen general anti-avoidance rules (GAAR) and expand tax authorities' purview to collect taxes retrospectively on the indirect transfer of shares have created concerns and uncertainties for foreign investors. A coordinated international effort to dissuade the government from implementing these laws in 2012 resulted in a one-year reprieve that may be extended to 2016. Private industry remains hopeful the Government of India will follow through with promises to overhaul India's direct and indirect tax regime. In 2009, the Government of India announced its intention to implement a Goods and Services Tax (GST) and streamline its Direct Tax Code (DTC). GST seeks to standardize taxes levied at all points in the supply chain concurrently by both the central and state governments.

A GST would replace and harmonize India under one tax regime by eliminating national and state Value-Added Taxes (VATs), central excise taxes, and a number of other state-level taxes. Parliamentary gridlock and uneven support from the state governments have stalled progress. GST is considered by many economists to be one of the most critical reforms the government could undertake. Some economists estimate that moving to GST could increase India's GDP growth by 2%.

Exports

In August 2009, MOCI released its foreign trade policy for fiscal years 2009-14, which highlighted various incentives for exporters with a particular emphasis on labor intensive sectors such as textiles, processed foods, leather, gems and jewelry, tea, and handloom-made items.

The duty credit extended to exporters under this scheme is 3% of the free-on-board (FOB) export value. Exporters are also allowed to import machinery and capital goods duty free. More information can be found here: http://dgft.gov.in/

RIGHT TO PRIVATE OWNERSHIP AND ESTABLISHMENT

Foreign and domestic private entities are allowed to establish and own businesses in trading companies, subsidiaries, joint ventures, branch offices, project offices, and liaison offices, subject to certain sector-specific restrictions. The Government of India does not permit investment in real estate by foreign investors, except for company property used to do business and for the development of most types of new commercial and residential properties. FIIs can now invest in Initial Public Offerings (IPOs) of companies engaged in real estate. They can also participate in pre-IPO placements undertaken by such real estate companies without regard to FDI stipulations.

To establish a business, various government approvals and clearances are required including incorporation of the company and registration under the State Sales Tax Act and Central and State Excise Acts' zoned area; obtain environmental site approval; seek authorization for electricity and financing; and obtain appropriate approvals for construction plans from the respective state and municipal authorities. Promoters also need to obtain industry-specific environmental approvals in compliance with the Water and Air Pollution Control Acts. Petrochemical complexes, petroleum refineries, cement thermal power plants, bulk drug makers, and manufacturers of fertilizers, dyes, and paper, among others, must obtain clearance from the Ministry of Environment and Forests.

PROTECTION OF PROPERTY RIGHTS

The Foreign Exchange Management Regulations and the Foreign Exchange Management Act set forth the rules that allow foreign entities to own immoveable property in India and convert foreign currencies for the purposes of investing in India. These regulations can be found (http://rbi.org.in/scripts) and (http://www. rbi.org.in/scripts/fema.aspx).

A foreign investment via the automatic route is allowed the same rights as a citizen for the purchase of immovable property in India in connection with an approved business activity.

India has adequate copyright laws, but enforcement is weak and piracy of copyrighted materials is widespread. India is a party to the Berne Convention, UNESCO, and the World Intellectual Property Organization (WIPO). In 2012,

India amended its copyright laws and signed WIPO's Beijing Treaty on the Protection of Audiovisual Performances.

However, the copyright law still contains several broad exceptions for personal use and "fair dealing," weak protection against unlawful circumvention of technological protection measures, and lacks an effective notice and take-down system for online infringing materials.

India updated its trademark law in recent years to bring it closer to international standards for filing and granting trademarks. India's Intellectual Property Office plans to implement trademark application filing under the Madrid Protocol in 2013.

This means that a single application can be used to register a trademark in any of the 84 member countries of the Madrid Protocol.

Pharmaceutical and agro-chemical products can be patented in India. Plant varieties are protected by the Plant Varieties and Farmers' Rights Act. Software embedded in hardware may also be patented. However, the interpretation and application of the patent law lacks clarity, especially with regard to several important areas such as: compulsory license, pre-grant opposition provisions, and defining the scope of patentable inventions (e.g., whether patents are limited to new chemical entities rather than incremental innovation).

In 2012, India issued its first compulsory license for a patented pharmaceutical. In the case of Natco vs. Bayer, an Indian generics company called Natco sought and was granted a compulsory license under India's laws to make a generic version of Bayer's kidney drug, Nexavar. Indian law does not protect against the unfair commercial use of test data or other data submitted to the government during the application for market approval of pharmaceutical or agro-chemical products.

The Pesticides Management Bill (2008), which would allow data protection of agricultural chemical provisions, is stalled in Parliament.

Indian law provides no statutory protection of trade secrets. The Designs Act meets India's obligations under TRIPS (Trade-Related Aspects of Intellectual Property Rights) for industrial designs.

The Designs Rules, which detail classification of design, conform to the international system and are intended to take care of the proliferation of design-related activities in various fields.

India's Semiconductor Integrated Circuits Layout Designs Act is based on standards developed by WIPO; however, this law remains inactive due to the lack of implementing regulations.

Transparency of the Regulatory System

Despite progress, the Indian economy is still constrained by excessive rules and an overly complex bureaucratic system that has broad discretionary powers. India has a decentralized federal system of government in which states possess extensive regulatory powers. Regulatory decisions governing important issues such as zoning, land-use, and the environment vary between states. Opposition from labor unions and political constituencies slows the pace of reform in land acquisition, environmental clearances, investment policy, and labor rights.

The Central government has been successful in establishing independent and effective regulators in telecommunications, securities, insurance, and pensions. The Competition Commission of India (CCI), India's antitrust body, has started using its enforcement powers and is now taking cases against cartelization and abuse of dominance, as well as conducting capacity-building programs. In December 2012, the Government of India introduced amendments to the Competition Act 2002 that would empower CCI to order search and seizure operations. Currently the commission's investigation wing is required to seek the approval of the local chief metropolitan magistrate for a search and seizure operation. In June 2011, the government enacted rules governing mergers and acquisitions. The Securities and Exchange Bureau of India (SEBI) enforces corporate governance and is well regarded by foreign institutional investors.

In December 2012, the Lok Sabha (Lower House of Parliament) approved the Companies Bill 2011, which replaces the Companies Act 1956. The Bill brings India's corporate governance rules in line with international standards. One aspect of the Bill that concerns foreign investors is a new mandatory rotation of audit partners. The Bill is pending approval from India's Rajya Sabha (Upper House of Parliament) and a pro-forma authorization from the President before it will be in force.

Efficiency of Capital Markets and Portfolio Investment

Indian capital markets are growing. The combined market capitalizations of the Bombay Stock Exchange (BSE) and the National Stock Exchange (NSE) surpassed USD 2.4 trillion in mid-November 2012. Lower than expected GDP growth in India is often linked to the decline in the Indian benchmark index Sensex that is trading nearly 30% lower than its peak in January 2008. Together, the NSE and BSE account for 100% of total Indian stock market turnover. According to the World Federation of Exchanges, both the BSE and NSE rank among the top 10 bourses in the Asia-Pacific region in terms of market capitalization of the companies listed on their platforms. Spot prices for index stocks are usually market-driven and settlement mechanisms are in line with international standards. India's debt and currency markets lag behind its equity markets. Although private placements of corporate debt have been increasing, daily trading volume remains low.

Foreign portfolio investment and activities in India's capital markets are regulated by a complex and onerous foreign institutional investor (FII) regime, analogous to China's Qualified Foreign Institutional Investor regime. The FII regime sets caps on investment and the scope of business. It reflects India' relatively closed capital account, the lack of market access for foreign firms, and the strict regulation of the financial sector.

FIIs investing in India's capital markets must register with SEBI, India's Securities and Exchange Commission (SEC) equivalent. They are divided into two categories: regular FIIs, which invest in both equity and debt; and 100% debt-fund FIIs. The list of eligible FIIs includes pension funds, mutual funds, banks, foreign central banks, sovereign wealth funds, endowment and university funds, foundations, charitable trusts and societies, insurance companies, re-insurance companies, foreign government agencies, international or multilateral organizations, broad-based funds, asset management companies, investment managers and hedge funds. FIIs must be registered and regulated by a recognized authority in their home country, meaning many US-based hedge funds cannot register as FIIs. FII registration can be made either as an investor or investor on behalf of its "accounts." "Sub-account" means any person residing outside India on whose behalf investments are made within India by an FII. As of March 2012, there are a total of 1,765 FIIs registered in India and 6,322 sub-accounts.

FIIs invested about USD 140 billion in India in 2011-12. While FIIs are allowed to invest in all securities traded on India's primary and secondary markets, unlisted domestic debt securities, and commercial paper issued by Indian companies, the Government of India imposes some restrictions based on investment type. As of November 2012, the allowed limit for FII investment in domestic debt instruments is USD 65 billion. Of this, USD 45 billion is earmarked for investment in corporate bonds and the remaining USD 20 billion is earmarked for investment in government securities. On November

30, the Finance Minister announced an increase in FII limits in government securities and corporate bonds by $5 billion each, taking the total investment limit in domestic debt to USD 75 billion. The RBI is expected to release detailed guidelines soon. In the equities market, FII and sub-accounts can own up to 10% and 5%, respectively, of the paid-up equity capital of any Indian company. Aggregate investment in any Indian company by all FIIs and sub-accounts is also capped at 24%, unless specifically authorized by that company's board of directors. "Naked short selling" is not permitted. FIIs are not permitted to participate in the new currency futures markets. Foreign firms and persons are prohibited from trading in commodities. SEBI allows foreign brokers to work on behalf of registered FIIs. FIIs can also bypass brokers and deal directly with companies in open offers. FII bank deposits are fully convertible and their capital, capital gains, dividends, interest income, and any compensation from the sale of rights offerings, net of all taxes, may be repatriated without prior approval. NRIs are subject to separate investment limitations. They can repatriate dividends, rents, and interest earned in India and their specially designated bank deposits are fully convertible.

Qualified Foreign Investors (QFIs) are allowed to invest in the equity and debt schemes of mutual funds and equities. QFIs are defined as individuals, groups, or associations that reside in a Financial Action Task Force (FATF)-compliant foreign country, a country that is a signatory to the International Organization of Securities Commissions' (IOSCO) multilateral Memorandum of Understanding, or a signatory of a bilateral MoU with SEBI. Limits on individual and aggregate investment for QFIs are 5% and 10% of the company's paid-up capital, respectively. These limits are over and above the cap earmarked for foreign institutional investors (FIIs) and non-resident individuals (NRIs), who can invest directly in the Indian equity market.

Foreign Venture Capital Investors (FVCIs) need to register with SEBI to invest in Indian firms. They can also set up a domestic asset management company to manage the fund. All such investments are allowed under the automatic route, subject to SEBI and RBI regulations and FDI policy. FVCIs can invest in many sectors including software business, information technology, pharmaceutical and drugs, bio-technology, nano-technology, biofuels, agriculture, and infrastructure.

Companies incorporated outside India can raise capital in India's capital market through the issuance of Indian Depository Receipts (IDRs). These transactions are subject to SEBI monitoring per the following conditions: www.rbi.org.in/Scripts/NotificationUser.aspx?Id=5185&Mode=0. Companies are required to have pre-issued, paid-up capital and have free reserves of least

USD 100 million, as well as an average turnover of USD 500 million during the three financial years preceding the issuance. In addition, the company must have been profitable for at least five years preceding the issuance, declaring dividends of not less than 10% each year and maintaining a pre-issue debt-equity ratio of not more than 2:1. Standard Chartered Bank, a British bank which was the first foreign entity to list in India in June 2010, is the only firm to have issued IDRs. In July 2011, a SEBI directive placed restrictions on conversion of actively traded IDRs in shares. The new SEBI directive describes illiquidity as an annualized turnover for the previous six months that is less than 5% of the total numbers of IDRs issued.

External Commercial Borrowing (ECB or direct lending to Indian entities by foreign institutions and non-banking finance companies) is allowed if the funds will be used for outward FDI or domestically for investment in industry, infrastructure, hotels, hospitals, or software. ECBs may not be used for on-lending, working capital, financial assets, or acquiring real estate or a domestic firm. In December 2012, the RBI allowed developers/builders for low cost affordable housing projects and housing finance companies who finance owners of low cost housing units, and micro finance institutions and non-government organizations engaged in micro finance activities to avail themselves of ECBs. As of December 2012, the all-in-costs ceilings for ECBs with an average maturity period of three to five years was capped at 350 basis points over six month LIBOR and 500 points for loans maturing after five years. As the cost of credit is significantly less in overseas markets, Indian companies have borrowed close to USD 27.8 billion in foreign currency through ECBs and FCCBs in the January-October 2012 period, of which USD 17 billion was via the automatic route. Takeover regulations require disclosure upon acquisition of shares exceeding 5% of total capitalization. SEBI regulations require that any acquisition of 15% or more of the voting rights in a listed company will trigger a public offer. The public offer made by the acquiring entity (i.e., an individual, company, or other legal entity) must be for at least 20% of the company's voting rights. Since October 2008, an owner holding between 55% and 75% of voting rights can acquire additional voting rights of up to 5% without making a public offer (i.e., creeping acquisition). However, the buyer can make a creeping acquisition only by open market purchases and not through bulk/block/negotiated deals or preferential allotment. Furthermore, subsequent to this acquisition, the buyer's total shares should not cross the 75% threshold. RBI and FIPB clearances are required to assume a controlling stake in an Indian company. Cross shareholding and stable shareholding are not prevalent in the Indian market. SEBI regulates hostile takeovers.

COMPETITION FROM STATE-OWNED ENTERPRISES (SOEs)

India's public sector enterprises (PSEs), both at the central and state levels, play an important role in the country's industrialization. As of 31st May 2012, there were as many as 249 CPSEs (excluding 7 insurance companies). The number of profit making Central Public Sector Enterprises (CPSEs) increased steadily from 143 CPSEs in 2004-05 to 160 CPSEs in 2010-11. The manufacturing sector constitutes the largest component of investment in CPSEs (45%) followed by services (35%), electricity (12%), and mining (8%). Foreigners are allowed to invest in these sectors. The Ministry of Heavy Industries and Public Enterprises' Department of Public Enterprises oversees CPSEs. CPSEs have a Board of Directors, wherein at least one third of the directors should be externally appointed without being promoters or relatives of promoters. The chairman, managing director, and directors are appointed independently. Companies can appoint private consultants, senior retired officers, and politically affiliated individuals to their boards. A detailed CPSE guideline on corporate governance is listed in this website: dpe.nic.in/newsite/gcgcpse2010.pdf.

As of 2011, the government had granted five CPSEs - Indian Oil Corporation, NTPC Limited, Oil and Natural Gas Corporation, Coal India Limited (CIL) and Steel Authority of India - "Maharatna" status, which allows the management greater financial and operational freedom to expand the CPSE's operations. Maharatna-designated CPSEs are allowed to invest up to USD 1.1 billion without government approval. The government plans to continue divesting itself of CPSEs, but intends to retain at least 51% ownership. Foreign investors are allowed to buy equity stakes in Maharatna and Navratna status companies via IPOs.

Although there do not appear to be systemic advantages, CPSEs in some sectors enjoy pricing and bidding advantages over their private sector and foreign competitors. Over the last few years the government has increased the pace of reducing its equity ownership in CPSEs, although there are no plans to sell majority shares of CPSEs to the private sector or to list more than 50% of the shares on any of the Indian stock exchanges.

CORPORATE SOCIAL RESPONSIBILITY (CSR)

The passage of the Companies Bill will mark a dramatic change in corporate social responsibility because the law includes a minimum requirement of spending on CSR activities companies are expected to meet. Once passed, the new legislation encourages publicly-held companies to spend 2% of annual their profits on CSR-related activities. In the proposed contribution guidelines that accompany the Bill, companies generating USD 200 million or more in sales, with a net worth greater than USD 100 million, and that have earned annual profits greater than USD 1 million for three consecutive years must report their CSR expenditures or provide an explanation of why the company did not meet the minimum-voluntary CSR spending recommendation. Companies that do not report could be subject to penalties. New guidelines following the passage of the Companies Bill passage have not yet been released on the Ministry's website and CSR activities are not defined in the draft legislation. While there is wide-spread support for encouraging more CSR activities in India, some companies have expressed concern about the lack of clarity and enforcement of the rules proposed in the Bill.

Foreign companies operating in India should verify if they are subject to the Ministry of Corporate Affairs' "National Voluntary Guidelines on Social, Environmental & Economic Responsibilities of Business," which encourages large companies to voluntarily spend 2% of their profits on corporate social responsibility (CSR) activities. The guidelines also require companies to disclose details regarding their CSR-related expenditures: www.mca.gov.in /Ministry/latestnews/National_Voluntary_Guidelines_2011_12jul2011.pdf

In 2012, Microsoft India was a semifinalist in the annual Secretary of State's Award for Corporate Excellence because of its significant contributions to improving environmental awareness in India.

NGO's working in India on CSR includes:

- ICCSR, the Indian Centre for Corporate Responsibility http:// www.iccsr.org/
- Transparency International India (TII) http://www.transparency india.org/

TII sponsors the Advocacy and Legal Action Center, which runs an Anti-Corruption Hotline and provides training sessions on corporate governance and CSR.

POLITICAL VIOLENCE

There were no reported politically motivated attacks on U.S. companies operating in India in 2012.

In Andhra Pradesh, protests, strikes, and violence related to the creation of a separate Telangana state continued and seem likely to continue into the foreseeable future. Local groups lodged complaints and threatened protests against U.S. companies, such as Google and Facebook, following the release of the YouTube *Innocence of Muslims* video but no violence occurred. Communal tensions and violence in Hyderabad's Old City disrupted tourism and business in that area, but no U.S. companies were reported in the media to have been affected. Although the violence is restricted to certain areas and U.S. companies are generally not affected, city-wide strikes have the ability to interfere with operations.

There continue to be outbursts of violence related to insurgent movements in Jammu and Kashmir and similar events in some northeastern states. Maoist/Naxalite insurgent groups remain active in some eastern and central Indian states, including the rural areas of Bihar, Jharkhand, Chhattisgarh, West Bengal, and Orissa. Travelers to India are invited to visit the Department of State travel advisory website at: travel.state for the latest information and travel resources.

CORRUPTION

While India's struggle with fighting corruption has heavily influenced Parliamentary sessions, media, and the public debate over the last year, little concrete action has been taken to curb the problem. Anti-corruption activist Arvind Kejriwal launched a series of corruption allegations against some of India's richest and most high-profile individuals, including a senior cabinet minister, family members of the ruling party's leader, and the president of the leading opposition party. U.S. firms continue to point to corruption as the single greatest disincentive to doing business in India. In private conversations, foreign firms note the lack of transparency in the rules of governance, extremely cumbersome official procedures, and excessive and unregulated discretionary powers afforded to politicians and lower-level bureaucrats as major obstacles to investing in India.

India's ranked 94 out of 174 countries surveyed in Transparency International's Corruption Perception Index in 2012. India's ranking, despite the national attention on the issue of combating corruption, was nearly identical to the previous year's ranking of 95 out of 183 countries. The legal framework for fighting corruption is addressed by the following laws: the Prevention of Corruption Act, 1988; the Code of Criminal Procedures, 1973; the Companies Act, 1956; the Indian Contract Act, 1872; and the Prevention of Money Laundering Act, 2002. Anti-corruption laws amended since 2004, granted additional powers to vigilance departments in government ministries at the central and state levels and raised India's Central Vigilance Commission (CVC) to be a statutory body. In May 2011, the GOI ratified the United Nations Convention against Corruption. In 2011, the Prime Minister had set an ambitious Parliamentary agenda to pass legislation intended to curb corruption. His arsenal of Bills aimed at reducing corruption included laws to create a national anti-corruption ombudsman, protect whistleblowers, eliminate corruption in government procurement, punish bribery of foreign public officials, address grievances against poor or corrupt delivery of government services and amendments to *the Prevention of Money Laundering Act* designed to expand the definition of money laundering. Most of these bills, however, remain stalled in Parliament.

The national Right to Information Act, 2005, and equivalent state acts function similarly to the U.S. Freedom of Information Act, requiring government officials to furnish information requested by citizens or face punitive action. The increased computerization of services, coupled with central and state government efforts to establish vigilance commissions, is opening up avenues to seek redress for grievances.

BILATERAL INVESTMENT AGREEMENTS

As of July 2012, India had concluded 82 bilateral investment agreements, including with the United Kingdom, France, Germany, Switzerland, Malaysia, and Mauritius. Of these, 72 are already in force. The complete list of agreements can be found at: http://www.finmin.nic.in/bipa/bipa_index.asp. In early 2012, media reported that Coal India lost in arbitration against an Australian firm. The Australian firm reportedly won its case based on more favorable treaty language from a third country investment treaty. Since this ruling, several more cases are rumored to be in process. In February 2011, India signed Comprehensive Economic Cooperation Agreements (CEPAs)s with Japan and Malaysia. In 2009, India concluded a CEPA with ASEAN and a free trade agreement (FTA) in goods, services, and investment with South Korea. FTA negotiations with the EU and Canada are still under way and India is negotiating a CEPA with Thailand. In June 2012, the U.S. and India held the fourth round of Bilateral Investment Treaty (BIT) negotiations. India continues to seek social security totalization agreement with the United States. India recently concluded a totalization agreement with Canada. India has totalization agreements with Belgium, France, Germany, Switzerland, the Netherlands, Hungary, the Czech Republic, Denmark, and Luxembourg. The U.S. Department of Commerce's International Trade Administration's "Invest in America" program and "Invest India," a joint venture between DIPP and the Federation of Indian Chambers of Commerce and Industry, signed a Memorandum of Intent in November 2009, to facilitate FDI in both countries. India and the United States have a double taxation avoidance treaty.

OPIC AND OTHER INVESTMENT INSURANCE PROGRAMS

The United States and India signed an Investment Incentive Agreement in 1987, which covers Overseas Private Investment Corporate (OPIC) programs. OPIC is currently operating in India in the areas of renewable energy and power, telecommunications, manufacturing, housing, services, education, clean water and logistics in infrastructure, and could support an additional USD 200 million or more in 2013, in clean energy and other projects in India. OPIC's total exposure in India is approximately USD 1.69 billion.

LABOR

Although there are more than 20 million unionized workers in India, unions represent less 5% of the total work force. Most unions are linked to political parties. According to provisional figures from the Ministry of Labor, 2 million work-days were lost to strikes and lockouts during the first nine months of 2012, as opposed to 10 million work-days lost in 2011, and 20 million in 2010, a marked improvement. Labor unrest occurs throughout India, though the reasons and affected sectors vary widely. India's largest car manufacturer Maruti Suzuki experienced violent strikes in 2012. The company was forced to shut down for a month leading to estimated losses around USD

300 million. In 2011, foreign companies in the manufacturing sector, such as General Motors, experienced labor problems in Gujarat, while others in the same sector report excellent labor relations. Some labor problems are the result of workplace disagreements over pay, working conditions, and union representation. Sometimes unrest is related to local political conditions beyond the companies' control. The states of Gujarat, Kerala, Andhra Pradesh, Karnataka, and Rajasthan experience the most strikes and lockouts, according to government statistics. Sectors with the most labor unrest include banks, excluding insurance and pension, and the automobile industry. India's labor regulations are among the world's most stringent and complex, and limit the growth of the formal manufacturing sector. The rules governing the payment of wages and salaries are set forth in the Payment of Wages Act, 1936, and the Minimum Wages Act, 1948. Industrial wages vary by state, ranging from about USD 3.50 per day for unskilled workers to over USD 200 per month for skilled production workers. Retrenchment, closure, and layoffs are governed by the Industrial Disputes Act, 1947, which requires prior government permission to lay off workers or close businesses employing more than 100 people. Permission is not easily obtained, resulting in a high use of contract workers in the manufacturing sector to circumvent the law. Private firms successfully downsize through voluntary retirement schemes. Foreign banks also require RBI approval to close branches. In August 2010, Parliament passed the Industrial Disputes (Amendment) Bill, 2010, which contains several provisions that: increase the wage ceiling prescribed for supervisors; bring disputes between contractors and contracted labor under the purview of the Ministry of Labor in consultation with relevant state or central government offices; provide direct access for workers to labor courts or tribunals in case of disputes; seek more qualified officers to preside over labor courts or tribunals; establish a grievance process; and empower industrial tribunals-cum-courts to enforce decrees.

FOREIGN TRADE ZONES/FREE TRADE ZONES

The GOI established several foreign trade zone schemes to encourage export-oriented production. These include Special Economic Zones (SEZ), Export Processing Zones (EPZ), Software Technology Parks (STP), and Export Oriented Units (EOU). The newest category is the National Industrial and Manufacturing Zones, of which there are 14 being established across India. These schemes are governed by separate rules and granted different benefits, details of which can be found at: www.sezindia.nic.in; www.stpi.in; and www.eouindia.gov.in/handbook_procedures.htm. SEZs are treated like foreign territory and therefore, businesses operating in SEZs are not subject to customs regulations, are not bound by FDI equity caps, receive exemptions from industrial licensing requirements, and enjoy tax holidays and other tax breaks. EPZs are industrial parks with incentives for foreign investors in export-oriented businesses. STPs are special zones with similar incentives for software exports. Export Oriented Units (EOUs) are industrial companies established anywhere in India that export their entire production and are granted: duty-free import of intermediate goods; income tax holidays; exemption from excise tax on capital goods, components, and raw materials; and a waiver of sales taxes. As part of its new industrial policy, the Government of India has started to establish National Investment and Manufacturing Zones (NIMZ). Nine NIMZs are already in the planning stages and will be established as green-field integrated industrial townships with a minimum area of 5000 hectares. The NIMZ will be managed by a special purpose vehicle, headed by a government official. The available information about NIMZ suggests that foreign and domestic companies that establish their operations in a NIMZ will be able to seek government authorizations via a single approval 'window' for all clearances.

FOREIGN DIRECT INVESTMENT STATISTICS

Table A. Inflow of FDI by top 5 countries (USD million)
[FY is April 1 to March 31]

Year	2007-08	2008-09	2009-10	2010-11	2011-12	2012-13*
TOTAL	24,581	27,331	25,888	21,383	35,121	14,788
Mauritius	11,096	11,229	10,376	6,987	9,942	6,757
Singapore	3,073	3,454	2,379	1,705	5,257	1,248
U.S.A.	1,089	1,802	1,943	1,170	1,115	323
U.K.	1,176	864	657	2711	7,874	611
Netherlands	695	883	899	1,213	1409	1,058
FDI/GDP(%)	2.4	3.2	3.7	1.6	2	

GDP is taken at factor cost.

* indicates FDI inflows for April 2012- October 2012 only.

Source: Secretariat for Industrial Assistance, Ministry of Commerce and Industry, GOI.

Table B. Inflow of FDI by top 5 countries (Rs billion) [FY is April 1 to March 31]

Year	2007-08	2008-09	2009-10	2010-11	2011-12	2012-13*
TOTAL	987	1230	1231	973	1,651	804
Mauritius	445	508	497	318	467	367
Singapore	123	157	113	77	247	68
U.S.A.	44	80	92	53	53	17
U.K.	47	38	31	122	364	32
Netherlands	28	39	43	55	66	57
FDI/GDP(%)	2.4	3.2	3.7	1.6	2	

GDP is taken at factor cost

* indicates FDI inflows for April 2012- October 2011 only.

Source: Secretariat for Industrial Assistance, Ministry of Commerce and Industry, GOI.

Table C. FDI Inflows by Sector - Top 5 (USD millions)

Sector	April 2000 - October 2012	2012-13*
All Services (fin and non-fin)	35,952	3600
Computers/Software	11,456	251
Telecommunication	12,601	48
Construction - Development - townships, housing and built-up infrastructure including roads	21,430	691

* indicates data is for April - October 2012 only (FY is April 1 to March 31)

Source: Secretariat for Industrial Assistance, Ministry of Commerce and Industry, GOI.

Table D. FDI Inflows by Sector - Top 5 (Rps billion)

Sector	April 2000 - October 2012	2012-13*
All Services (fin and non-fin)	1,653	195
Computers/Software	514	13
Telecommunication	573	2
Construction - Development - townships, housing and built-up infrastructure including roads	975	37

* indicates data is for April – October 2012 only (FY is April 1 to March 31).

Source: Secretariat for Industrial Assistance.

In: Brazil, Russia, India, China, and South Africa   ISBN: 978-1-62618-627-9
Editor: Sandra C. Owens   © 2013 Nova Science Publishers, Inc.

Chapter 4

2013 INVESTMENT CLIMATE STATEMENT: CHINA[*]

Bureau of Economic and Business Affairs

OPENNESS TO, AND RESTRICTIONS UPON, FOREIGN INVESTMENT

China attracted USD 124 billion in foreign direct investment (FDI) in 2011, second only to the United States. China's sustained high economic growth rate and the expansion of its domestic market help explain its attractiveness as an FDI destination. However, foreign investors often temper their optimism regarding potential investment returns with uncertainty about China's willingness to offer a level playing field vis-à-vis domestic competitors. In addition, foreign investors report a range of challenges related to China's current investment climate. These include industrial policies that protect and promote state-owned and other domestic firms, equity caps and other restrictions on foreign ownership in many industries, weak intellectual property rights (IPR) protection, a lack of transparency, corruption, and an unreliable legal system.

China has a legal and regulatory framework that provides the government with discretion to promote investment in specific regions or industries it wishes to develop, and to restrict foreign investment deemed not to be in its

---

[*] This is an edited, reformatted and augmented version of Bureau of Economic and Business Affairs publication, dated February 2013.

national interest or that might compete with state-sanctioned monopolies or other favored domestic firms. Foreign investors report that many regulations contain undefined key terms and standards, and that regulations are often applied in an inconsistent manner by different regulatory entities and localities. Potential investment restrictions in China are thus much broader than those of many developed countries, including the United States.

Investment Policies

The Chinese government has stated that it welcomes foreign investment. In particular, China seeks to promote investment in higher value-added sectors, including high technology research and development, advanced manufacturing, clean energy technology, and select modern services sectors. Export-oriented investments also often receive government support. A major goal of China's investment policies is to encourage the domestic development of technological innovation and know-how. Investment projects that involve the transfer of technology or the potential for "indigenous innovation" tend to be favorably received by China's investment authorities. Foreign investors have said they must often weigh China's market potential and its interest in attracting technology against China's inability or unwillingness to protect investors' intellectual property.

China has indicated that it plans to restrict foreign investment in resource-intensive and highly-polluting industries, citing some kinds of basic manufacturing as an example. In addition, China appears to discourage foreign investments in sectors: 1) where China seeks to develop domestic firms into globally competitive multinational corporations; 2) that have benefited historically from state-sanctioned monopolies or from a legacy of state investment; or 3) deemed key to social stability. It also discourages investments that are intended to profit from currency, real estate, or asset speculation.

China seeks to spread the benefits of foreign investment beyond its relatively wealthy coastal areas by encouraging foreign companies to establish regional headquarters and operations in Central, Western, and Northeastern China. China publishes and regularly revises a *Catalogue of Priority Industries for Foreign Investment in the Central-Western Regions*, which outlines incentives to attract investment in targeted sectors to those parts of China.

Five-Year Plan

China defines its broad economic goals through five-year macro-economic plans. The most significant of these for foreign investors is China's Five-Year Plan (FYP) on Foreign Capital Utilization. *The 12th FYP for Utilization of Overseas Capital and Investment Abroad*, issued by the National Development and Reform Commission (NDRC), promises to guide more foreign direct investment (FDI) to an identified set of strategic and newly emerging industries (SEIs), while "strictly" limiting FDI in energy and resource-intensive and environmentally damaging industries; encourage foreign multinationals to set up regional headquarters and research and development (R&D) centers in China; encourage foreign investment in production services such as modern logistics, software development, engineering design, vocational skill training, information consulting, technology, and intellectual property services; "steadily open up" banking, securities, insurance, telecom, fuel, and logistics industries; "gradually open up" education and sports; guide foreign capital to enter healthcare, culture, tourism, and home services; and encourage foreign capital to enter creative design. The plan aims to accelerate the introduction and utilization of international innovation resources and further integrate the Chinese innovation system with the global innovation network so as to promote and strengthen indigenous innovation capacities and the shift in the economic growth model. Support measures include supporting foreign-invested firms to team up with domestic firms or research institutions to apply for national R&D programs and innovation capacity building programs, and for certification of national technology centers; establishing an IPR review system to support R&D; promoting fair competition between foreign and domestic firms; and strengthening IP protection, among other things.

Catalogue for the Guidance of Foreign Investment in Industries

China outlines its specific foreign investment objectives primarily through its *Catalogue for the Guidance of Foreign Investment in Industries*, most recently revised in December 2011. The catalogue delineates sectors of the economy where foreign investment is "encouraged," "restricted," and "prohibited." Investment in sectors not listed in the catalogue is considered permitted. China "encourages" investment in sectors where it believes it will benefit from foreign assistance or technology. Investment is "restricted" and "prohibited" in sectors that China deems sensitive, that touch on national security, or which do not meet the goals of China's economic development plans. The catalogue also notes many sectors where equity caps limit foreign ownership, often to a minority share, giving Chinese partner-firms significant control and allowing them to benefit from technology transfer.

Problems with the Catalogue

The catalogue reflects China's market access restrictions. Contradictions between the catalogue and other measures have confused investors and added to the perception that investment guidelines do not provide a secure basis for business planning. Even in "encouraged" and "permitted" sectors, regulations apart from the catalogue often detail additional restrictions on the specific forms of investment that are allowed. Chinese regulators have maintained the flexibility to ignore the catalogue's guidance in some instances, and to restrict or approve foreign investment for reasons other than those specified. The government may also adopt new regulations or establish industrial policies that supersede the most recently published edition of the catalogue. Uncertainty as to which industries are being promoted and how long such designations will be valid undermines confidence in the stability and predictability of the investment climate.

China's Foreign Investment Approval Regime

According to the *Interim Measures for the Administration of Examining and Approving Foreign Investment Projects*, issued in October 2004 and still in effect, all proposed foreign investment projects in China must be submitted for "verification" and approval to the National Development and Reform Commission (NDRC) or to provincial or local Development and Reform Commissions, depending on the sector and value of the investment. *The (For-Comment Draft) Measures for the Administration of Verification of Foreign Investment Projects*, issued by NDRC in August 2012, would codify the easing of foreign investment "verification" criteria so that only investments of above $300 million in the "encouraged" and "permitted" categories (up from a previous threshold of $100 million), and above $50 million in the "restricted" category, would be subject to NDRC "verification." The new draft measures also add "security review" as one item for review and would require, when necessary, solicitation of public opinion if a project could have an adverse effect on the public interest. NDRC's approval process includes assessing the project's compliance with China's laws and regulations, its national security implications, and its economic development ramifications. In some cases, NDRC also solicits the opinions of relevant Chinese industrial regulators and "consulting agencies," which may include industry associations that represent domestic firms. The State Council may also weigh in for high-value projects in "restricted" sectors.

Once NDRC approves a project, investors apply to the Ministry of Commerce (MOFCOM) for approval to legally establish a company. MOFCOM (or, depending on the sector and value of the investment, the provincial or local Department of Commerce) is responsible for three types of review: 1) a general review of all proposed foreign investment in China (including both greenfield investment projects, as well as mergers and acquisitions); 2) an anti-monopoly review of certain proposed mergers and acquisitions; and 3) a security review of certain proposed mergers and acquisitions. Foreign investors next apply for a business license from the State Administration of Industry and Commerce (SAIC), which allows the firm to operate. Once a license is obtained, the investor registers with China's tax and foreign exchange agencies. Greenfield investment projects must also seek approval from China's Environmental Protection Ministry and its Ministry of Land Resources.

The actual implementation of China's foreign investment approvals process may vary in specific cases, depending on the details of a particular investment proposal and local rules and practices.

Mergers and Acquisitions and the Anti-Monopoly Law

MOFCOM's Anti-Monopoly Bureau reviews mergers and acquisitions (M&A) above a certain threshold and meeting certain criteria specified in China's Anti-Monopoly Law (AML). While the AML calls for evaluation of the merger's effect on competition, it also allows antitrust regulators to consider factors beyond consumer welfare, such as national security and other issues deemed relevant to national economic development. The AML states that China will protect the "lawful activities" of state-regulated monopolies and state-owned enterprises (SOEs).

As of the end of September 2012, MOFCOM's Anti-Monopoly Bureau accepted 562 cases and has completed 510, among which 487 (95 percent) were unconditionally approved while 15 transactions were approved with conditions. Twelve of the M&A cases approved with conditions involved offshore transactions between foreign parties. As of September 2012, MOFCOM's Anti-Monopoly Bureau had dealt with three American acquisitions of Chinese companies, rejecting one and approving the others.

Problems with China's Foreign Investment Approval Regime and the Anti-Monopoly Law

All proposed foreign investments in China are evaluated on a case-by-case basis, allowing significant discretion on the part of Chinese regulators to impose unexplained restrictions on new investment projects and to take into account the interests of domestic competitors. This ad hoc system diminishes the transparency of China's investment regulations and adds to investor uncertainty. Although the law does not expressly state that joint ventures fall under its scope, MOFCOM requires joint ventures to submit notification under the AML. AML implementation also suffers from lengthy review timelines and a lack of decision-making transparency. MOFCOM decisions to block or conditionally clear proposed M&A transactions are the only administrative decisions required to be publicized. In Fall 2012, MOFCOM released a list of 458 M&A cases unconditionally approved during the period August 2008 to the end of September 2012.

Merger & Acquisition Security Review

In February 2011, China released the *State Council Notice Regarding the Establishment of a Security Review Mechanism for Foreign Investors Acquiring Domestic Enterprises*. The notice established an interagency Joint Conference, led by NDRC and MOFCOM, with the authority to block foreign mergers and acquisitions of domestic firms that it believes may have an impact on national security. The Joint Conference is instructed to consider not just national defense security but also national economic security and basic social order implications when reviewing transactions. Some provincial and municipal departments of commerce have posted on the Internet a Security Review Industry Table that lists industries not related to defense, which are potentially subject to this review mechanism; however, MOFCOM has declined to confirm that this list reflects official Chinese policy.

Investment Restrictions in "Vital Industries and Key Fields"

The December 2006 *Guiding Opinions Concerning the Advancement of Adjustments of State Capital and the Restructuring of State-Owned Enterprises* called on China to consolidate and develop its state-owned economy, including enhancing its control and influence in "vital industries and key fields relating to national security and national economic lifelines." The document defined "vital industries and key fields" as "industries concerning national security, major infrastructure and important mineral resources, industries that provide essential public goods and services, and key enterprises in pillar industries and high-tech industries."

At the time the document was published, the Chairman of the State-owned Assets Supervision and Administration Commission (SASAC) listed industries in which the state should maintain "absolute control" (aviation, coal, defense, electric power and the state grid, oil, and petrochemicals, shipping, and telecommunications) and "relative control" (automotive, chemical, construction, exploration and design, electronic information, equipment manufacturing, iron and steel, nonferrous metal, and science and technology). China maintains that these lists do not reflect its official policy. In some cases, more than fifty percent ownership in some of these industries has been permitted on a case-by-case basis, especially if a particular expertise or technology is deemed important at the time.

China's State Assets Law is intended to safeguard China's economic system, promote the "socialist market economy," fortify and develop the state-owned economy, and enable SOEs to play a leading role in China's economy, especially in "vital industries and key fields." The law requires China to adopt policies to encourage SOE concentration and dominance in industries vital to national security and "national economic security."

Additional Laws Related to Foreign Investment

China's State Secrets Law gives the government broad authority to classify information as a "state secret," creating uncertainty and potential risk for investors negotiating with SOEs or operating in sensitive sectors. The Contract Law encourages contractual compliance by providing legal recourse for a breach of contract, although enforcement of judgments continues to be a problem. Additional investment-related laws include, but are not limited to: the Administrative Permissions Law; the Arbitration Law; the Corporate

Income Tax Law; the Enterprise Bankruptcy Law; the Foreign Trade Law; the Government Procurement Law; the Insurance Law; the Labor Contract Law; the Law on Import and Export of Goods; and the Securities Law.

Rankings

The following table lists China's most recent rankings by organizations that monitor economies' economic freedom, business regulations, and perceived level of corruption.

Indicator	Year	Score	Rank
Transparency International Corruption Perceptions Index	2011	3.6/10	75/183
Heritage Foundation and Wall Street Journal Index of Economic Freedom	2011	52/100	135/183
World Bank Ease of Doing Business Index	2012	N/A	91/183

Conversion and Transfer Policies

Foreign-invested enterprises in China do not need pre-approval to open foreign exchange accounts and are allowed to retain income as foreign exchange or convert it into renminbi without quota requirements. Foreign exchange transactions on China's capital account no longer require a case-by-case review by the State Administration of Foreign Exchange (SAFE). Instead, designated foreign exchange banks review and directly conduct foreign exchange settlements.

The Chinese government registers all commercial foreign debt and limits foreign firms' accumulated medium and long-term debt from abroad to the difference between total investment and registered capital. Foreign firms must report their foreign exchange balance once per year.

Expropriation and Compensation

Chinese law prohibits nationalization of foreign-invested enterprises except under "special" circumstances. Chinese officials have said these circumstances include national security and obstacles to large civil engineering projects, but the law does not define the term. Chinese law requires compensation of expropriated foreign investments but does not describe the formula to be used in calculating the amount. The Department of State is not aware of any cases since 1979 in which China has expropriated a U.S. investment, although the Department has notified Congress of several cases of concern.

Dispute Settlement

Chinese officials typically urge firms to resolve disputes through informal conciliation. If formal mediation is necessary, Chinese parties and the authorities typically promote arbitration over litigation. Many contracts prescribe arbitration by the China International Economic and Trade Arbitration Commission (CIETAC). Some foreign parties have obtained favorable rulings from CIETAC, while others question CIETAC's procedures and effectiveness. Other arbitration commissions exist and are usually affiliated with the government at the provincial or municipal level. For contracts involving at least one foreign party, offshore arbitration may be adopted.

Arbitration awards are not always enforced by Chinese local courts. Investors may appeal to higher courts in such cases.

Formal commercial disputes between investors are heard in economic courts. In practice, China's court system is not independent of the government, and the government often intervenes in disputes. Corruption may also influence local court decisions and local officials may disregard the judgments of domestic courts. China's legal system rarely enforces foreign court judgments.

Reports of business disputes involving violence, death threats, hostage-taking and travel bans involving Americans continue to increase, although American citizens and foreigners in general do not appear to be more likely than Chinese nationals to be subject to this treatment. Police are often reluctant to intervene in what they consider to be internal contract disputes.

Investor-state disputes leading to arbitration are rare in China. China has never lost an arbitration case resulting from an investment dispute. China is a member of the International Center for the Settlement of Investment Disputes (ICSID) and has ratified the United Nations Convention on the Recognition and Enforcement of Foreign Arbitral Awards (the New York Convention).

Performance Requirements and Incentives

China has committed to eliminate export performance, trade and foreign exchange balancing, and local content requirements in most sectors. China has also committed to enforce only technology transfer rules that do not violate World Trade Organization (WTO) standards on intellectual property and trade-related investment measures.

In practice, however, local officials and some regulators prefer investments that develop favored industries and support the local job market. Provincial and municipal governments often restrict access to their local markets, government procurement, and public works projects even to firms that have invested in the province or municipality. In addition, Chinese regulators have reportedly pressured foreign firms in some sectors to disclose intellectual property content or license it to competitors, sometimes at below market rates.

Many localities – including special economic zones, development zones and science parks – court foreign investors with packages of reduced income taxes, resource and land use fees, and import/export duties, as well as priority treatment in obtaining basic infrastructure services, streamlined government approvals, and funding support for start-ups.

These packages may also stipulate export, local content, technology transfer, or other requirements.

Right to Private Ownership and Establishment

In China, all commercial enterprises require a license from the government. There is no broad right to establish a business. Disposition of an enterprise is also tightly regulated. The Administrative Permissions Law requires reviews of proposed investments for conformity with Chinese laws and regulations and is the legal basis for China's complex approval system for foreign investment.

Protection of Property Rights

The Chinese legal system mediates acquisition and disposition of property. Chinese courts have an inconsistent record in protecting the legal rights of foreigners.

Tangible Property Rights

All land in China is owned by the state. Individuals and firms, including foreigners, can own and transfer long-term leases for land, structures, and personal property, subject to many restrictions. China's Property Law stipulates that residential property rights will be automatically renewed while commercial and industrial grants shall be renewed absent a conflicting public interest. A number of foreign investors have seen their land-use rights revoked as neighborhoods are slated by the government for development. Investors report compensation in these cases has been nominal.

China's Securities Law defines debtor and guarantor rights and allows mortgages of certain types of property and other tangible assets, including long-term leases as described above. Foreigners can buy non-performing debt through state-owned asset management firms, but bureaucratic hurdles limit their ability to liquidate assets.

Intellectual Property Rights

China acceded to the World Intellectual Property Organization (WIPO) Copyright Treaty and the WIPO Performances and Phonograms Treaty in 2007. China is also a member of the Paris Convention for the Protection of Industrial Property, the Berne Convention for the Protection of Literary and Artistic Works, the Madrid Trademark Convention, the Universal Copyright Convention, and the Geneva Phonograms Convention, among other conventions.

China has updated many of its laws and regulations to comply with the Agreement on Trade-Related Aspects of Intellectual Property Rights (TRIPS). However, there are still aspects of China's IPR regime that the United States believes fall short of international best practices, and, if improved, would provide greater protection to intellectual property. Industry associations representing software, entertainment, consumer goods, and others continue to report high levels of IPR infringement in China. Trademark and copyright violations are widespread, and U.S. companies and industry associations report increasing concerns related to patent infringement, and bad faith trademark registration as well. A recent increase in cases involving the theft of trade secrets in China, as well as cases of trade secret theft that occur outside China for the benefit of Chinese entities, also demonstrate that there is a systemic lack of effective protection and enforcement of IPR. During its "Special IPR

Campaign" from October 2010 through June 2011, China emphasized criminal prosecutions against IPR violations, particularly in the copyright area. In general, however, criminal penalties for infringement are not applied on a frequent and consistent enough basis to significantly deter ongoing infringement. Furthermore, administrative sanctions are typically non-transparent and are so weak as to also lack a deterrent effect. Because of relatively low damage awards, civil litigation against IPR infringements continues to be of limited effect.

Significant regional differences exist in IPR infringement and enforcement, with some areas showing higher levels of IPR protection and enforcement, while there are reports of others offering safe harbors to local trademark counterfeiters and copyright pirates. While many Chinese officials are increasing enforcement efforts, infringement generally continues to outpace enforcement. Lack of coordination among various government agencies also continues to hamper many enforcement efforts. Although China announced the creation in November 2011 of a permanent, State-Council-led IPR enforcement office to coordinate intellectual property protection at the national level, with corresponding organizations serving this role in provinces and municipalities, the United States continues to encourage the further implementation of systemic enhancements to the protection and enforcement of IPR in order to significantly reduce levels of IPR-infringement in China.

Transparency of the Regulatory System

China's legal and regulatory system is complex and generally lacks consistent enforcement. Foreign investors rank inconsistent and arbitrary regulatory enforcement and lack of transparency among the major problems they face in China's market.

The State Council's Legislative Affairs Office (SCLAO) has issued instructions to Chinese agencies to publish all foreign trade and investment related laws, regulations, rules, and policy measures in the MOFCOM Gazette, in accordance with China's WTO accession commitment. In addition, it has also issued notices to require its own departments and other central government agencies to post proposed economic-related regulatory policies on the official SCLAO website for public comment. Although SCLAO posts many proposed regulations and draft rules on its website for public comment, often for no less than 30 days, many central government ministries and agencies still only post a limited number of draft trade and economic-related departmental rules on their own ministry websites for public comment. Comment periods can be extremely brief, and the impact of public comments on final regulations is not clear.

Moreover, there are an increasing number of regulatory policies for which public comment is not sought before they are finalized. Foreign investors report that Chinese regulators at times rely on unpublished internal guidelines that nonetheless affect their businesses.

State actions motivated by a perceived need to protect social stability or achieve other political goals can affect foreign investors. Access to foreign online resources, including news, cloud-based business services, and virtual private networks (VPNs), is often and increasingly restricted without official acknowledgement or explanation. Foreign-invested companies have also reported threats of retaliation by the government for actions taken by the U.S. and other foreign governments at the WTO and in regards to outward Chinese investment.

Efficient Capital Markets and Portfolio Investment

Bank loans continue to provide the majority of credit in China, although other sources of capital, such as corporate bonds, trust loans, equity financing, and private equity financing are expanding their scope, reach and sophistication. Regulators use administrative methods, such as reserve requirements, lending quotas, and loan-to-deposit ratios, to control credit growth.

The People's Bank of China (PBOC), China's central bank, allowed some flexibility in mid-2012 for banks to set deposit and lending rights. This has squeezed the net interest margin of banks (i.e., the gap between deposit and lending rates), which has cut into the profits of China's banking sector. Favored borrowers, particularly SOEs, benefit from greater access to capital and lower financing costs, as lenders perceive these entities to have an implicit government guarantee and hence lower risk profiles. Small- and medium-sized enterprises (SMEs), by contrast, experience the most difficulty obtaining bank financing, instead financing investments through retained earnings or informal channels, including other Chinese firms or private lenders. The Chinese government has expressed concerns over the potential risks that China's "shadow banking" poses to the financial sector and has implemented pilot programs, for example in Wenzhou city, to encourage private capital to move into official channels that can be monitored and regulated.

Non-bank financing has expanded over the last few years, including through public listing of stock, either inside or outside of China, and more firms are issuing debt. Most foreign portfolio investment in Chinese companies occurs on foreign exchanges, primarily in New York and Hong Kong. In addition, China has significantly expanded quotas for certain foreign institutional investors to invest in domestic stock markets. Direct portfolio investment by private equity and venture capital firms is also rising rapidly, although from a small base.

Competition from State-Owned Enterprises

China's leading SOEs benefit from preferential government policies and practices aimed at developing bigger and stronger national champions. SOEs enjoy administrative monopolies over the most essential economic inputs (land, hydrocarbons, finance, telecoms, electricity) and considerable power in the markets for others (steel, minerals). SOEs have long enjoyed preferential access to credit. According to some Chinese academics, provincial governments have used their power to manipulate industrial policies to deny operating licenses in order to persuade reluctant owners to sell out to bigger state-owned suitors.

China has two sovereign wealth funds: The China Investment Corporation (CIC) and SAFE. CIC is overseen by a board of directors and a board of supervisors. SAFE is a government agency that reports directly to the PBOC. The SAFE Administrator serves concurrently as a PBOC Vice Governor. CIC and SAFE invest a very limited amount of their funds domestically. The funds are required neither to submit their books to independent audit nor to publish annual reports, although CIC issued its first annual report in 2009.

Corporate Social Responsibility

Corporate social responsibility (CSR), or what is increasingly known as sustainability, is a relatively new concept for domestic companies in China and is less widely accepted there than in the United States. Investors looking to partner with Chinese companies or expand operations with Chinese suppliers face challenges ensuring domestic firms meet internationally recognized, voluntary industry standards in such areas as labor, the environment, and good manufacturing practices. China's 12th Five-Year Plan highlights sustainability issues as a means to draw attention to the subject. Foreign-invested enterprises tend to follow generally accepted CSR principles, and most report annually on their CSR policies and achievements.

Political Violence

The risk of political violence directed at foreign companies operating in China remains small. Some violent but unconnected protests have occurred in all parts of China, but such mass incidents generally involved local residents protesting corrupt officials, environmental and food safety concerns, confiscated property, and wage disputes. In the fall of 2012, against a backdrop of rising tensions between China and Japan over territorial issues, some businesses owned or perceived to be owned by Japanese in multiple Chinese cities faced Chinese protests. Economic activity between China and Japan suffered as a result, but has since shown signs of recovery.

Corruption

Corruption remains endemic in China. Sectors requiring extensive government approval are the most affected, including banking, finance, and construction. The lack of an independent press, as well as the fact that all bodies responsible for conducting corruption investigations, are controlled by the Communist Party hamper anti-corruption efforts. Senior officials and family members are suspected of using connections to avoid investigation or prosecution for alleged misdeeds.

According to Chinese law, accepting a bribe is a criminal offense with a maximum punishment of life in prison or death in "especially serious" circumstances. The maximum punishment for offering a bribe to a Chinese official is five years in prison, except when there are "serious" or "especially serious" circumstances, when punishment can range from five years to life in prison. A February 2011 amendment to the Criminal Law made offering large bribes to foreign officials or officials of international organizations a punishable offense, although there has yet to be a prosecution.

The Supreme People's Procuratorate and the Ministry of Public Security investigate criminal violations of laws related to anti-corruption, while the Ministry of Supervision and the Communist Party Discipline Inspection Committee enforce ethics guidelines and party discipline. China's National

Audit Office also inspects accounts of state-owned enterprises and government entities.

China ratified the United Nations Convention against Corruption in 2005 and participates in Asia-Pacific Economic Cooperation (APEC) and Organization for Economic Cooperation and Development (OECD) anti-corruption initiatives. China has not signed the OECD Convention on Combating Bribery.

Bilateral Investment Agreements

China has bilateral investment agreements with over 100 countries and economies, including Austria, the Belgium-Luxembourg Economic Union, Canada, France, Germany, Italy, Japan, South Korea, Spain, Thailand, and the United Kingdom. China's bilateral investment agreements cover expropriation, arbitration, most-favored-nation treatment, and repatriation of investment proceeds. They are generally regarded as weaker than the investment treaties the United States seeks to negotiate.

The United States and China concluded a bilateral taxation treaty in 1984. In the fall of 2012, the United States resumed negotiation of a bilateral investment treaty.

OPIC and Other Investment Insurance Programs

The United States suspended Overseas Private Investment Corporation (OPIC) programs in the aftermath of China's crackdown on Tiananmen Square demonstrators in June 1989. OPIC honors outstanding political risk insurance contracts.

The Multilateral Investment Guarantee Agency, an organization affiliated with the World Bank, provides political risk insurance for investors in China. Some foreign commercial insurance companies also offer political risk insurance, as does the People's Insurance Company of China.

Labor

Human resource issues remain a major concern for American companies operating in China. Difficulties in hiring appropriately skilled labor, navigating many new and often ill-defined labor and social safety net laws, restrictions on the mobility of workers, and the lack of independent trade unions combine to create a challenging environment for foreign-invested enterprises.

Independent trade unions are illegal in China. Officially sanctioned trade unions must affiliate with the All-China Federation of Trade Unions (ACFTU), which is an arm of the Communist Party. It is illegal for employers to oppose efforts to establish ACFTU unions. While worker protests and work stoppages occur regularly, the right to strike is not protected by law.

China has not ratified core International Labor Organization conventions on freedom of association and collective bargaining, but has ratified conventions prohibiting child labor and employment discrimination. Apart from a lack of freedom of association and the right to strike, Chinese labor laws generally meet international labor standards. However, enforcement of existing labor regulations is inconsistent and poor.

Foreign Trade Zones/Free Trade Zones

China's principal bonded areas include Shanghai, Tianjin, Shantou, three districts within Shenzhen (Futian, Yantian and Shatoujiao), Guangzhou, Dalian, Xiamen, Ningbo, Zhuhai, and Fuzhou. Besides these official duty-free zones identified by China's State Council, numerous economic development zones and open cities offer similar privileges and benefits to foreign investors.

Foreign Direct Investment Statistics

Data Limitations

Investment from and to some economies, including but not limited to the British Virgin Islands, the Cayman Islands, Hong Kong, and Macau, may mask the ultimate source/destination of the investment. Some analysts have noted that investment from and to Taiwan may be underreported.

Chinese FDI data do not include much of the high dollar-value minority equity stakes that American financial services firms have taken in major Chinese lenders.

In addition, China does not classify reinvested locally-generated profits as new investment.

FDI as a Percentage of Gross Domestic Product

According to the United Nations Conference on Trade and Development, China's FDI stock equaled 16 percent of its gross domestic product (GDP) in 2011; China's FDI inflows equaled 2 percent of GDP.

Foreign Direct Investment Flows for 2011 (Top 10 Sources of Origin)

Country/Economy of Origin	Millions of U.S. Dollars
Hong Kong	70,500
British Virgin Islands	9,725
Japan	6,330
Singapore	6,097
South Korea	2,551
United States	2,369
Cayman Islands	2,242
Taiwan	2,183
Samoa	2,076
Mauritius	1,139

Source: China Commerce Yearbook 2012.

Cumulative* Foreign Direct Investment for 2011 by Selected Source of Origin

Country/Economy of Origin	Millions of U.S. Dollars
Hong Kong	788,396
British Virgin Islands	121,571
Japan	79,895
United States	67,592
Taiwan	54,199
South Korea	49,854
Singapore	52,956
Cayman Islands	23,830
Germany	18,311
United Kingdom	17,666

Source: China Commerce Yearbook 2012.

*Cumulative values are totals of the data collected each year, are not adjusted for inflation, and do not account for divestment.

Flow of Outbound Direct Investment for 2011 (Top 10 Destinations)

Destination	Millions of U.S. Dollars
Hong Kong	35,654
British Virgin Islands	6,208
Cayman Islands	4,936
France	3,482
Singapore	3,269
Australia	3,165
United States	1,811
UK	1,420
Luxembourg	1,265
Sudan	912

Source: China Commerce Yearbook 2012.

Stock of Outbound Direct Investment for 2011 (Top 10 Destinations)

Destination	Millions of U.S. Dollars
Hong Kong	261,519
British Virgin Islands	29,261
Cayman Islands	21,692
Australia	11,041
Singapore	10,602
United States	8,993
Luxembourg	7,082
South Africa	4,060
Russia	3,764
Canada	3,728

Source: China Commerce Yearbook 2012.

Web Resources

Chinese Government
- Chinese Embassy in Washington, D.C.: http://www.china-embassy. org/eng/
- Ministry of Commerce: http://english.mofcom.gov.cn/;
- Invest in China: http://www.fdi.gov.cn/pub/FDI_EN/default.htm

- National Development and Reform Commission: http://en.ndrc.gov. cn/
- State Administration of Foreign Exchange: http://www.safe.gov.cn/
- State Administration of Taxation http://www.chinatax.gov.cn/ n6669073/index.html

United States Government

- U.S. Embassy in Beijing (Doing Business in China): http://beijing.usembassy-china.org.cn/business.html
- U.S. Department of State travel information: http://travel.state.gov/
- U.S. Trade Representative: http://www.ustr.gov/
- U.S. Department of Commerce: http://www.export.gov/
- U.S. Department of the Treasury: http://www.treasury.gov/Pages/ default.aspx
- Export Import Bank: http://www.exim.gov/
- Overseas Private Investment Corporation (OPIC): http://www.opic. gov/
- U.S. Trade and Development Agency: http://www.ustda.gov/

2012 Non-Governmental Reports on China's Investment Climate

- U.S. Chamber of Commerce's *China's Approval Process for Inbound Foreign Direct Investment*: http://www.uschamber.com/sites/default/ files/reports/020021_China_InvestmentPaper_hires.pdf
- AmCham China's 2012 *Business Climate Survey*: http://www. amchamchina.org/businessclimate2012
- European Chamber *Business Confidence Survey 2012*: http://www. europeanchamber.com.cn/en/publications-business-confidence-survey-2012

In: Brazil, Russia, India, China, and South Africa   ISBN: 978-1-62618-627-9
Editor: Sandra C. Owens   © 2013 Nova Science Publishers, Inc.

Chapter 5

2013 INVESTMENT CLIMATE STATEMENT: SOUTH AFRICA[*]

Bureau of Economic and Business Affairs

OPENNESS TO FOREIGN INVESTMENT

The government of South Africa is open to green field foreign investment as a means to drive economic growth, improve international competitiveness, and access foreign export markets. Merger and acquisition activity is more sensitive and requires more advance work. Virtually all business sectors are open to foreign investment. Certain sectors require government approval for foreign participation, including energy, mining, banking, insurance, and defense. Excepting those sectors, no government approval is required to invest, and there are few restrictions on the form or extent of foreign investment. The Department of Trade and Industry's (DTI) Trade and Investment South Africa (TISA) division provides assistance to foreign investors. The DTI concentrates on sectors in which research has indicated that the foreign country has a comparative advantage. TISA offers information on sectors and industries, consultation on the regulatory environment, facilitation for investment missions, links to joint venture partners, information on incentive packages, assistance with work permits, and logistical support for

---

[*] This is an edited, reformatted and augmented version of Bureau of Economic and Business Affairs publication, dated February 2013.

relocation. DTI publishes the "Investor's Handbook" on its website: www.dti.gov.za. DTI expects to release the 2012 publication in January 2013.

While the South African government supports investment in principle, investors and market commentators were concerned its commitment to assist foreign investors was insufficient in practice. Some of their concerns included a belief that the national-level government lacked a sense of urgency when it came to supporting investment deals. Several investors reported trouble accessing senior decision makers. Additionally, South Africa has begun scrutinizing merger- and acquisition-related foreign direct investment for its impact on jobs and local industry. Private sector representatives and other interested parties were concerned about politicization of South Africa's posture towards this type of investment.

Macroeconomic management was generally strong over the past decade, with reduced levels of public debt, generally low inflation, and a positive rate of economic growth until the global slowdown in 2009. While inflation increased during 2012, it remained within the central bank's target range of 3-6 percent. As growth stalled, however, government revenue has been negatively affected to result in a projected deficit of 4.3 percent of GDP through March 2013; although, worse-than-expected third and fourth quarter GDP results could push the deficit higher. While still investment worthy, South African sovereign debt was downgraded in 2012. In September, Moody's downgraded South Africa's credit rating to Baa1 from A3, and maintained a negative outlook. The rating agency cited the government's weakening institutional strength, lackluster economic growth despite low interest rates, infrastructure shortfalls, high labor costs despite high unemployment, and increased concern about political stability. This brought Moody's rating into line with Fitch Ratings. Standard and Poor's downgraded South Africa further to BBB in October, the lowest rating of all three major rating agencies.

Since the end of apartheid in 1994, the government has liberalized trade and enhanced international competitiveness by lowering tariffs, abolishing most import controls, undertaking some privatization and reforming the regulatory environment. While this resulted in several large foreign acquisitions in banking, telecommunications, tourism and other sectors, foreign direct investment has fallen short of the government's expectations. South African banks are well capitalized and have little exposure to sub-prime debt or other sources of financial contagion. Moody's in December 2012, however, downgraded the outlook for South African banks to negative based on their holding of government securities and overall weak macroeconomic conditions.

South Africa's Industrial Policy Action Plan (IPAP) aims to strengthen industrial infrastructure development. Key stated objectives include revising government procurement policy to support targeted sectors (capital and transport equipment; automotive; chemical, plastic fabrication and pharmaceuticals; and forestry, paper and furniture); using trade and competition policy to improve South Africa's competitiveness; and facilitating industrial financing for small- and medium-sized firms.

Mergers and acquisitions in South Africa are subject to screening and approval under the Competition Act of 1998. This act allows South Africa's Competition Commission to review investment for public interest considerations such as its effect on specific industrial sectors, employment within South Africa, the ability of small businesses to become competitive, and the ability of national industries to compete internationally. These broad powers present a risk. Political interference has, at times, imposed requirements that discriminated against foreign investors. The Competition Tribunal reviews decisions made by the Competition Commission. Inward investment is subject the Companies Act of 2011, which sets out requirements for corporate governance, among other considerations. See the "Transparency of the Regulatory System" section of this report for more about South Africa's Companies Act.

South Africa's Broad-Based Black Economic Empowerment (B-BBEE) program has a significant effect on foreign investment. B-BBEE is an affirmative action program assisting historically disadvantaged South Africans to participate in the economy. B-BBEE requirements are specified in the Codes of Good Practice, which were published in the Government Gazette in 2007. The codes, first implemented in 2011, created a Black Economic Empowerment (BEE) "Scorecard" to rate a firm's commitment to economic transformation using seven different dimensions—ownership, management, skills development, employment equity, preferential procurement, enterprise development, and socio-economic development. Each dimension is weighted, with ownership receiving the most empowerment points (20) and socio-economic development the least (5). Equity equivalence deals provide multinational corporations options for scoring on the ownership dimension without the transfer of equity stakes, which could run against the company's bylaws. Such a deal would likely involve creation of a black-owned South African joint venture valued at least 25 percent of the multinational's South African operations. However, the process for approving an equity equivalent mechanism by the DTI is complicated and requires a significant effort on the part of the multinational. Two U.S. companies have established equity equivalence schemes since 2007. Other companies have scored sufficiently well without such a scheme by focusing their transformation efforts on B-BBEE dimensions other than ownership.

In addition to B-BBEE transformation framework, sectors such as financial services, mining, and petroleum have their own "transformation charters" intended to accelerate empowerment within the sector. In 2011, the integrated transport, forest products, construction, tourism, and chartered accountancy sectors had force of law in South Africa. In 2012, the Information and Communication Technology (ICT) Charter and Property Sector and Financial Services Charters gained force of law. Other sectors, including Agri-business and Marketing, have transformation charters that are more "aspirational" in nature.

In October 2012, the government submitted for public comment proposed revisions to the law underpinning its B-BBEE policy. The revisions emphasize local procurement and introduce measures to combat the practice of "fronting," by which companies manipulate or misrepresent their black empowerment levels to win contracts.

The government reasoned an increased focus on enterprise and skill development over simple equity ownership would produce more meaningful transformation of the South African economy. The revisions also introduced penalties for companies failing to perform sufficiently across all key dimensions, including ownership, which would make certification more difficult for multinationals.

The government has argued a more rigorous scoring regime was necessary to ensure only those firms most committed to economic transformation gain the benefits of B-BBEE certification.

The public comment period ended December 5, and after further review the government may forward draft amendments to the National Assembly sometime in 2013.

Openness Index

South Africa is not a Millennium Challenge Corporation (MCC) compact country. Therefore, it is not ranked by MCC on measures of openness. The following chart lists South Africa's ranking in other widely used indices compiled by non-governmental organizations.

Measure	Year	Index/Ranking
Transparency International Corruption Index	2012	69
Heritage Economic Freedom	2012	70
World Bank Doing Business	2012	35

Currency Conversion and Transfer Policies

The South African Reserve Bank's (SARB) Exchange Control Department administers foreign exchange policy. An authorized foreign exchange dealer, normally one of the large commercial banks, must handle international commercial transactions and report every purchase of foreign exchange, irrespective of the amount. Generally, there are only limited delays in the conversion and transfer of funds. Due to South Africa's relatively closed exchange system, no private player, however large, can hedge large quantities of Rand for more than five years.

While non-residents may freely transfer capital in and out of South Africa, transactions must be reported to authorities. Non-residents may purchase local securities without restriction. To facilitate repatriation of capital and profits, foreign investors should ensure an authorized dealer endorses their share certificates as "non-resident." Foreign investors should also be sure to maintain an accurate record of investment.

Subsidiaries and branches of foreign companies in South Africa are considered South African entities and are treated legally as South African companies. As such, they are subject to exchange control by the SARB. South African companies may, as a general rule, freely remit the following to non-residents: repayment of capital investments; dividends and branch profits (provided such transfers are made out of trading profits and are financed without resorting to excessive local borrowing); interest payments (provided the rate is reasonable); and payment of royalties or similar fees for the use of know-how, patents, designs, trademarks or similar property (subject to prior approval of SARB authorities).

While South African companies may invest in other countries without restrictions, SARB approval/notification is required for investments over R500 million. South African individuals may freely invest in foreign firms listed on South African stock exchanges. Individual South African taxpayers in good standing may make investments up to a total of R4 million in other countries. As of 2010, South African banks are permitted to commit up to 25 percent of their capital in direct and indirect foreign liabilities. In addition, mutual and other investment funds can invest up to 25 percent of their retail assets in other countries. Pension plans and insurance funds may invest 15 percent of their retail assets in other countries.

Before accepting or repaying a foreign loan, South African residents must obtain SARB approval. The SARB must also approve the payment of royalties and license fees to non-residents when no local manufacturing is involved. When local manufacturing is involved, the DTI must approve the payment of royalties related to patents on manufacturing processes and products. Upon proof of invoice, South African companies may pay fees for foreign management and other services provided such fees are not calculated as a percentage of sales, profits, purchases, or income.

SARB approval is required for the sale of all forms of South African-owned intellectual property rights (IPR). Approval is generally granted by SARB if the transaction occurs at arm's length and at fair market value. IPR owned by non-residents is not subject to any restrictions in terms of repatriation of profits, royalties, or proceeds from sales.

Further questions on exchange control may be addressed to:

South African Reserve Bank
Exchange Control Department
P.O. Box 427, Pretoria, 0001
Tel: +27 (0) 12 313-3911; Fax: +27 (0) 12 313-3197
Website: http://www.reservebank.co.za/

Expropriation and Compensation

The Expropriation Act of 1975 (Act) and the Expropriation Act Amendment of 1992 entitles the government to expropriate private property for reasons of public necessity or utility. The decision is an administrative one. Compensation should be the fair market value of the property as agreed between the buyer and seller, or determined by the court, as per section 25 of the Constitution. There is no record, dating back to 1924, of an expropriation or nationalization of a U.S. investment in South Africa.

Racially discriminatory property laws during apartheid resulted in highly distorted patterns of land ownership in South Africa. In 2011, South Africa tabled a "Green Paper" on land reform to address these distortions. The Green Paper's "three pillars" include a land management commission, a land valuer-general and a land rights management board with local management committees. These would keep track of land sales, ensure proper record keeping, and "facilitate productive land usage and an equitable land distribution." Certain provisions in the Green Paper have generated controversy such as proposed "severe limitations" on private land ownership, particularly foreign ownership, the powers granted to a proposed "valuer-general" to assist the Department of Rural Development and Land Reform in assessing the fair value of land, the proposed Commission's powers to invalidate title deeds and confiscate land, and the state's right to intervene regarding the use of land. As of late 2012, this paper had not yet been turned into draft legislation. The government, however, approved a motion to establish an Office of the Valuer-General in November 2012. This motion could be brought before the National Assembly in 2013 as a bill to be given the force of law.

In several restitution cases, in which the government initiated proceedings to expropriate white-owned farms after courts ruled the land had been seized from blacks during apartheid, the owners rejected the court-approved purchase prices.

In most of these cases, the government and owners reached agreement on compensation prior to any final expropriation actions. The government has twice exercised its expropriation power, taking possession of farms in Northern Cape and Limpopo Provinces in 2007 after negotiations with owners collapsed. The government paid the owners the fair market value for the land in both cases.

The Mineral and Petroleum Resources Development Act 28 of 2002 ("MPRDA"), enacted in May 2004, gave the state ownership of all of South Africa's mineral and petroleum resources. It replaced private ownership with a system of licenses controlled by the South African government. Under the MPRDA, investors who held pre-existing rights were granted the opportunity to apply for licenses provided they met certain criteria, including the achievement of certain BEE objectives.

Controversial debates over the nationalization of mines and banks continued at the highest political levels in South Africa throughout most of 2012. Proponents claim it would redistribute wealth and tackle economic inequality.

Critics argue nationalization is neither tenable nor workable in South Africa due to the potential cost of compensating mine owners and the broader, adverse impact it would have on foreign investment.

Dispute Settlement

South Africa is a member of the New York Convention of 1958 on the recognition and enforcement of foreign arbitration awards, but is not a member of the World Bank's International Center for the Settlement of Investment Disputes. South Africa recognizes the International Chamber of Commerce, which supervises the resolution of transnational commercial disputes. South Africa applies its commercial and bankruptcy laws with consistency, and has an independent, objective court system for enforcing property and contractual rights. South Africa's new Companies Act also provides a mechanism for Alternative Dispute Resolution. South African courts retain discretion to hear a dispute over a contract entered into under U.S. law and under U.S. jurisdiction. The South African court will interpret the contract with the law of the country or jurisdiction provided for in the contract, however.

Dispute resolution can be a time intensive process in South Africa. If the matter is urgent, and the presiding judge agrees, an interim decision can be taken within days while the subsequent appeal process can take months or years. If the matter is a dispute of law and is not urgent, it may proceed by application or motion to be solved within months. Where there is a dispute of fact, the matter is referred to trial, which can take several years. The Alternative Dispute Resolution involves negotiation, mediation or arbitration, and may resolve the matter within a couple of months. Alternative Dispute Resolution is increasingly popular in South Africa for many reasons, including the confidentiality which can be imposed on the evidence, case documents and the judgment.

Performance Requirements and Incentives

DTI offers several investment incentives for manufacturing:

- Business Process Services (BPS) replaced in 2010 the Business Process Outsourcing & Off-Shoring (BPO&O) investment incentive. BPS is aimed at attracting investment and creating employment in South Africa through off-shoring activities. The incentive consisted in 2011 of a tax exempt grant of R112,000 (US$12,600) paid over three years for each offshore job created and maintained. The value of the incentive declines in 2012 and 2013. Between FY13 and FY15, each job will net a grant worth R32,000 (US$3,600). There is an additional

20 percent incentive for creating 400-800 offshore jobs in a year, and 30 percent for more than 800 offshore jobs created. To qualify, companies must: be starting new operations or expanding existing BPS activities; must create at least 50 new off-shore jobs in South Africa within three years; and must commence operations no later than six months from the approval of the BPS incentive grant.

- The 12i Tax Incentive supports green field investments (i.e. new industrial projects that utilize only new and unused manufacturing assets), as well as brown field investments (i.e. expansions or upgrades of existing industrial projects). The 12i incentive is available for investments with a total value of more than R1.6 million (US$235,000). Projects must be within the priority sectors identified in the Industrial Policy Action Plan (IPAP). Projects should: upgrade an industry within South Africa; provide general business linkages within South Africa; acquire goods and services from small, medium and micro-sized enterprises (SMMEs); create direct employment within South Africa; provide skills development in South Africa; and, in the case of a Greenfield project, be located within an Industrial Development Zone (IDZ).

- The Manufacturing Investment Program offers local- and foreign-owned entities an investment grant of up to 30 percent of qualifying investment costs in machinery, equipment, commercial vehicles, land and buildings required for: establishing a new production facility; expanding an existing production facility; or upgrading production capability in an existing clothing and textile production facility.

- The Sector Specific Assistance Scheme (SSAS) is a reimbursable cost-sharing grant whereby financial support is provided to Export Councils, Industry Associations, and Joint Action Groups. Export Councils represent the trade promotion efforts of specific industries, while Industry Associations represent sectors DTI has prioritized for development. Joint Action Groups are groups of companies or associations cooperating on one-time projects in sectors prioritized for development by DTI. Foreign companies can access SSAS funding through participation in one of these entities.

- The Film and Television Production Rebate Scheme encourages foreign and domestic investment in the local film industry. Eligible applicants may receive a rebate of 15 percent of the production expenditures for foreign productions and up to 25 percent for qualifying South African productions. To qualify, film projects must have begun after 2004 and investment in the film must reach R25 million (approximately US$3.67 million). Other requirements include completing 50 percent of the principal photography in South Africa and a minimum of four weeks' local photography time. Eligible productions include movies, television series, and documentaries. The maximum rebate for any project will be R20 million (US$2.9 million U.S.).

- The Automotive Investment Scheme was announced in 2010 as part of the Automotive Production and Development Program (APDP). It provides qualifying firms a taxable cash grant of 20 percent of the value of qualifying investment in productive assets. To qualify, a light motor vehicle manufacturer must introduce a new or replacement model with a minimum 50,000 units of annual production per plant within three years. A component manufacturer can qualify by proving that a contract has been awarded for the manufacture of components for the light motor vehicle manufacturing supply chain, and that the investment will generate revenue of R10 million (US$1.4 million). An additional taxable cash grant of 5-10 percent is available if additional conditions are met. APDP stipulates that automobile import tariffs will be frozen at 25 percent until 2020.

- The Capital Projects Feasibility Programme (CPFP) is a cost-sharing grant that contributes to feasibility studies for projects to increase local exports and stimulate the market for South African capital goods and services. The cap on a feasibility study grant is R8 million or 50 percent of the total costs for projects outside Africa and 55 percent of the total costs for projects in Africa. A foreign entity will only be considered if it partners with a South African registered entity, and if the application is submitted by the South African entity.

- The Critical Infrastructure Programme (CIP) is a cost sharing grant for projects designed to improve critical infrastructure in South Africa. The grant covers qualifying development costs from a minimum of 10 percent to a maximum of 30 percent towards the total development costs of qualifying infrastructure. It is made available upon the completion of the infrastructure project concerned. Private firms with a minimum B-BBEE level of four can qualify.

- Incubation Support Programme (ISP) develops small, micro and medium enterprises (SMMEs incubators that create successful enterprises with the potential to revitalize communities and strengthen local and national economies. The program is available to applicants that want to establish new incubators or wish to grow and expand existing ones. Support is on a cost-sharing basis between the Government and private sector partner(s). It is available for infrastructure and business development services necessary to mentor and grow enterprises to ensure that within two to three years they achieve self-sustainability. The grant approval is capped at a maximum of R10 million (VAT inclusive) per financial year over a three year period and is subject to the availability of funds. The ISP offers a cost-sharing support of 50:50 for large businesses and a cost-sharing of 40:60 for SMMEs. Applicants can be a registered legal entity in South Africa in terms of the Companies Act, 1973 (as amended) or the Companies Act, 2008 (as amended); the Close Corporations Act, 1984 (as amended) or the Co-operatives Act, 2005 (as amended).

- The Manufacturing Competitiveness Enhancement Programme (MCEP) introduced in the Industrial Policy Action Plan (IPAP) 2012/13 – 2014/15 encourages manufacturers to upgrade production facilities in a manner that sustains employment and maximizes value-addition in the short to medium term. The MCEP Production Incentive (provides grants for five areas: Capital Investment; Green Technology and Resource Efficiency Improvement; Enterprise-Level Competitiveness Improvement grant; Feasibility Studies; and Cluster Interventions. The Industrial Financing and Loan Facilities offers: the Pre- and Post-Dispatch Working Capital Facility - a maximum of R30 million for up to four years, at a preferential fixed interest rate of percent; and the Industrial Policy Niche Projects Fund - DTI-identified projects with potential for job creation, diversification of manufacturing output and contribution to exports, and that would otherwise not be candidates for commercial or IDC funding. Applicants can be a registered legal entity in South Africa in terms of the Companies Act, 1973 (as amended) or the Companies Act, 2008 (as amended); the Close Corporations Act, 1984 (as amended) or the Co-operatives Act, 2005 (as amended).

- The Support Programme for Industrial Innovation (SPII) promotes technology development in South Africa's industry through financial assistance for the development of innovative products and/or processes. SPII focuses on the development phase, which begins at the conclusion of basic research and ends at the point when a pre-production prototype has been produced. There are three schemes

SPII uses to apply assistance. Assistance is linked to BEE levels. Criteria are that development and subsequent production takes place within South Africa; Intellectual Property to reside in South African registered company; and Participating businesses should (must) be South African registered enterprises.

- The Clothing and Textile Competitiveness Improvement Programme (CTCIP) builds capacity among manufacturers and the apparel value chain in South Africa on issues of cost, quality, flexibility, reliability, adaptability and the capability to innovate. The Production Incentive (PI) forms part of the overall Clothing and Textile Competitiveness Programme (CTCP) for the clothing, textiles, footwear, leather and leather goods industries.

Details on these and other investment programs are available at the DTI website at: www.dti.gov.za − Trade Exports and Investment − Incentives, or Financial Assistance − Industrial Development Incentives, or Industrial Development − Incentives.

South Africa's various provinces have development agencies that offer incentives to encourage investors to establish or relocate industry to their areas. The incentives vary from province to province and may include reduced interest rates, reduced costs for leasing land and buildings, cash grants for the relocation of physical plants and employees, reduced rates for basic facilities, railroads and other transport rebates, and assistance in the provision of housing. Under the National Industrial Participation Program (NIPP), foreign companies winning large government tenders exceeding US$10 million must invest at least 30 percent of the value of the imported content of the tender in South Africa.

Several South African public entities have been established to support investment in export-oriented industries, research and development, or offer technical assistance to industry:

- The Industrial Development Corporation (IDC) is a self-financing, state-owned corporation that provides equity and loan financing to support investment in target sectors. The IDC also provides credit facilities for South African exporters
- The Council for Scientific and Industrial Research (CSIR) is a government-owned organization that does multi-disciplinary research and development for industrial application.

- Technifin, a CSIR subsidiary, finances the commercialization of new technology and products.
- MINTEK develops mining and mineral processing technology for commercial application.
- The Council for Geoscience undertakes geological surveys and services related to minerals exploration. Foreign companies and research organizations can access research done by a specific organization through partnerships and direct contract.

South Africa uses government procurement policies to promote domestic economic development and fight unemployment. South Africa's Preferential Procurement Policy Framework Act of 2000 (the Framework Act) and associated implementing regulations created a legal framework and formula for evaluating tenders for government contracts. Certain provisions of the Act provide a pathway for government departments to issue tenders that favor local content providers. Moreover, in a bid to boost industrialization and to create jobs, the government signed with labor leaders in 2011 the "Local Procurement Accord," which commits the government to increasing the proportion of goods and services procured from South African suppliers to an "aspirational target" of 75 percent.

Right to Private Ownership and Establishment

The right to private property is protected under South African law. All foreign and domestic private entities may freely establish, acquire and dispose of commercial interests. The securities regulation code requires an offer to minority shareholders when 30 percent of shareholding has been acquired in a public company with at least ten shareholders and net equity in excess of R5 million.

Protection of Property Rights

The South African legal system protects and facilitates the acquisition and disposition of all property rights (e.g., land, buildings, and mortgages). Deeds must be registered at the Deeds Office. Banks usually register mortgages as security when providing finance for the purchase of property.

Owners of patents and trademarks may license them locally, but when a patent license entails the payment of royalties to a non-resident licensor, DTI must approve the royalty agreement. Patents are granted for twenty years - usually with no option to renew. Trademarks are valid for an initial period of ten years, renewable for ten-year periods. The holder of a patent or trademark must pay an annual fee to preserve ownership rights. All agreements relating to payment for the right to use know-how, patents, trademarks, copyrights, or other similar property are subject to approval by exchange control authorities in the SARB. A royalty of up to four percent of the factory selling price is the standard approval for consumer goods. A royalty of up to six percent will be approved for intermediate and finished capital goods.

Literary, musical, and artistic works, as well as cinematographic films and sound recordings are eligible for copyright under the Copyright Act of 1978. New designs may be registered under the Designs Act of 1967, which grants copyrights for five years.

The Counterfeit Goods Act of 1997 provides additional protection to owners of trademarks, copyrights, and certain marks under the Merchandise Marks Act of 1941. The Intellectual Property Laws Amendment Act of 1997 went into force on 1997. It amended the Merchandise Marks Act of 1941, the Performers' Protection Act of 1967, the Patents Act of 1978, the Copyright Act of 1978, the Trademarks Act of 1993, and the Designs Act of 1993 to bring South African intellectual property legislation fully into line with the WTO's Trade-Related Aspects of Intellectual Property Rights Agreement (TRIPS). Amendments to the Patents Act of 1978 also brought South Africa into line with TRIPS, to which South Africa became a party in 1999, and implemented the Patent Cooperation Treaty.

In August 2012, the Copyright Review Commission (CRC) released a report recommending amending laws to hold Internet Service Providers (ISPs) and Wireless Application Service Providers (WASPs) accountable for copyright violations occurring through the internet and improve royalty collection.

The CRC's recommendations should be proposed to parliament as bills in 2013. In September 2012, President Zuma referred back to the National Assembly for reconsideration a bill to amend four pieces of IP legislation to include protection of indigenous intellectual property. One potential source of concern was the legislation's vague definition of "indigenous" intellectual property, which could have undermined the ability of existing IP rights holders to protect their rights in court. President Zuma's decision, however, referred to questions of constitutional process.

Transparency of the Regulatory System

South African laws and registrations are generally published in draft form for stakeholder comment, and legal, regulatory, and accounting systems are generally transparent and consistent with international norms.

South Africa implemented a new Companies Act in 2011, intended to encourage entrepreneurship and employment opportunities by simplifying company registration procedures and reducing the costs for forming new companies. It is also intended to promote innovation and investment in South African markets and companies by providing for a predictable and effective regulatory environment. In the first action against a U.S. company under the new act, South Africa's Competition Appeals Court dismissed in March 2012 an appeal by the South African Government to overturn the Competition Tribunal's approval of a U.S. company's purchase of a majority stake in a South African retailer. The court, however, ordered the South African firm to re-employ 503 workers fired before the merger and commissioned a study to recommend the best means by which South African small and medium sized suppliers could participate in the U.S. company's global value chain.

South Africa's Consumer Protection Act (2008) went into effect in 2011. The legislation reinforces various consumer rights, including right of product choice, right to fair contract terms, and right of product quality. Impact of the legislation will vary by industry, and businesses will need to adjust their operations accordingly. The legislation for the Consumer Protection Act can be found at: www.dti.gov.za/ccrdlawreview/DraftConsumerProtectionBill.htm

The implementing regulations can be found at: www.dti.gov.za/ccrd/cpa_regulations.htm.

Efficient Capital Markets and Portfolio Investment

South African banks are well capitalized and comply with international banking standards. There are 17 registered banks in South Africa and 12 are branches of foreign banks. Four banks - Standard, ABSA, First Rand, and Nedbank - dominate the sector, accounting for almost 84 percent of the country's banking assets, which total over US$466 billion. The South African Reserve Bank (SARB) regulates the sector according to the Bank Act of 1990. There are three alternatives for foreign banks to establish local operations, all of which require SARB approval: separate company, branch, or representative office. The criteria for the registration of a foreign bank are the same as for domestic banks. Foreign banks must include additional information, such as holding company approval, a letter of "comfort and understanding" from the holding company, and a letter of no objection from the foreign bank's home regulatory authority. More information on the banking industry may be obtained from the South African Banking Association at the following website: www.banking.org.za/.

The Financial Services Board (FSB) governs South Africa's non-bank financial services industry (see website: www.fsb.co.za/). The FSB regulates insurance companies, pension funds, unit trusts (i.e., mutual funds), participation bond schemes, portfolio management, and the financial markets. The JSE Securities Exchange SA (JSE) is the seventeenth largest exchange in the world measured by market capitalization. Market capitalization stood at R7.267 billion (US$835 million) in October 2012, with 388 firms listed. The Bond Exchange of South Africa (BESA) is licensed under the Financial Markets Control Act. Membership includes banks, insurers, investors, stockbrokers, and independent intermediaries. The exchange consists principally of bonds issued by government, state-owned enterprises, and private corporations. The JSE acquired BESA in 2009. More information on financial markets may be obtained from the JSE (website: www.jse.co.za). Non-residents are allowed to finance 100 percent of their investment through local borrowing (previously, they were required to invest R1 for every R3 borrowed locally). A finance ratio of 1:1 also applies to emigrants, the acquisition of residential properties by non-residents, and financial transactions such as portfolio investments, securities lending and hedging by non-residents.

Competition from State-Owned Enterprises

State-owned enterprises (SOE) play a significant role in the South African economy. In key sectors such as electricity, transport (air, rail and freight), and telecommunications, SOEs play a lead role, often defined by law, although limited competition is allowed in some sectors. The government's interest in these sectors often competes with and discourages foreign investment. The Department of Public Enterprises has oversight responsibility in full or in part for nine of the approximately 300 SOEs that exist at the national, provincial and local levels: Alexcor (diamonds); Broadband Infraco (fiber optic cable); Denel (military equipment); Eskom (electricity generation); Pebble Bed Modular Reactor (nuclear); South African Airways; South African Air

Express; SAFCOL (forestry) and Transnet (transportation). Government oversight can inject some political uncertainty into business decisions. In November 2012, Standard and Poor's (S&P) downgraded seven large South African companies, including parastatals Telkom, Eskom and Transnet, and underscored a negative outlook for the corporate bond market by signaling more downgrades could follow. S&P cited problems in the global economy, economic policy uncertainty, and a weaker investment climate in South Africa.

Government plans to "ring-fence" Eskom's power purchasing function from its power generating function have not materialized. This hinders the advent of independent power producers (IPPs) in the energy market. Draft legislation to create an independent system and market operator (ISMO) remains under review after nearly two years, further limiting competition in the domestic energy market. South Africa's renewable energy program, however, registered a success in November when the government signed contracts with 28 IPPs to add 1,400MW of renewable energy generation capacity to the national grid. The renewable program aims to add 3725 MW of new generation capacity by 2016, contributing towards the long-term goal of creating over 17000 MW of renewable energy generation capacity by 2030.

In February 2012, President Jacob Zuma announced a major infrastructure investment strategy to address South Africa's unemployment and infrastructure needs. The Presidential Infrastructure Coordinating Commission (PICC) adopted the Infrastructure Plan, which outlines 17 Strategic Integrated Projects (SIPs) worth US$384 billion over a 20-year period. The SIPS are comprised of more than 150 individual projects spread throughout South Africa's nine provinces. The PICC's plan is separate from another major infrastructure initiative, Transnet's Market Demand Strategy (MDS), announced in April 2012. MDS will channel more than US$33.9 billion into port and rail infrastructure upgrades. Transnet is a state-owned company that manages the country's port, rail and pipeline networks.

Direct aviation links between the United States and Africa are limited, but have expanded over the past few years. The growth of low-cost carriers in South Africa has reduced domestic airfares, but private carriers are likely to struggle against national carriers without further air liberalization in the region and in Africa. In South Africa, the state-owned carrier, South African Airways (SAA), relies on the government for financial assistance to stay afloat. SAA dominates the southern Africa regional market, but faces competition from regional airlines such as Emirates. SAA underwent a contentious leadership change in late 2012 over public disagreements with the Department of Public Enterprises (DPE), its major shareholder.

While government efforts to liberalize the telecommunications sector and encourage competition have improved, regulatory uncertainty and fragmented competition have hampered growth. Key challenges include: strengthening the capacity of the sector regulator, the Independent Communications Authority of South Africa (ICASA), to implement a spectrum auction; ensuring digital migration remains on track; stabilizing the Department of Communication's state-owned companies, including Telkom (national telephone operator), the South African Broadcasting Company (SABC), and Sentech (signals provider); and improving broadband penetration. ICASA falls under the Department of Communications.

South Africa's telecommunications priority is effecting the migration from analogue to digital broadcasting. This will significantly improve South Africa's broadcast capabilities as frequencies occupied by analogue will become available for next-generation mobile broadband networks. Progress has been sporadic, however, leaving industry concerned South Africa will miss the global deadline of June 1, 2015. With four ministers since 2006, leadership stability in the Department of Communications has been one obstacle. Industry insiders also argue the Department of Communications lacks personnel who understand the digital migration process. Meanwhile, technology reviews and legal challenges hamper ICASA's ability to regulate.

Political Violence

Political violence is a growing problem in South Africa, primarily in KwaZulu Natal, where over 30 persons appear to have been killed in 2012 for political reasons. In 2011, South Africa's Independent Electoral Commission, with support from the South African Police Service, held municipal elections generally considered free and fair, despite minor voting irregularities, and violence was not a factor. Service delivery protests and strike actions are frequent and occasionally turn violent. There were a number of violent strikes in 2012, including among gold and platinum miners, and farmer workers of the Western Cape (see labor section).

Corruption

Allegations of corruption in the public tendering process persist in South Africa at all levels of government, despite the country's excellent anti-corruption regulatory framework, as highlighted by the Prevention and Combating of Corrupt Activities Act of 2004. In 2010 and 2011, the government intensified anti-corruption efforts. While the newly formed priority crimes unit, the "Hawks," is thus far less effective than the unit it replaced in 2009 (the "Scorpions"), it has arrested a number of white collar criminals for banking irregularities and fraud.

Bilateral Investment Agreements

South Africa has bilateral investment treaties (BITs) with 41 countries, including Argentina, Austria, Belgium and Luxemburg, Canada, Chile, the Czech Republic, Finland, France, Germany, Greece, Mauritius, the Netherlands, the Republic of Korea, Spain, Sweden, Switzerland, Turkey, and the United Kingdom. After a review of BITs began in 2010, the DTI determined in 2012 that "first generation" BITs, an estimated 30 agreements mostly with EU states, exposed South Africa or created domestic policy conflicts, and should be terminated. South Africa may adopt a new BIT model for the future that exempts investor-state dispute and expropriation provisions, and facilitates the government's economic transformation goals including Broad-based Black Economic Empowerment (B-BBEE). In September 2012, South Africa gave notice to Belgium and Luxemburg that it will terminate their BITs in March 2013, and informed the EU that remaining BITs would be allowed to expire. Article 52 of the 2000 EU-South Africa Trade, Development, and Cooperation Agreement covers investment promotion and protection.

The United States and South Africa signed a Trade and Investment Framework Agreement (TIFA) in 1999. TIFA discussions were renewed in 2011, and the agreement was updated in 2012. The United States and SACU negotiated a Trade, Investment and Development Cooperation Agreement (TIDCA), which was signed in 2008. The U.S.-South Africa bilateral tax treaty eliminating double taxation entered into force in 1998.

OPIC Programs

Since a 1993 agreement to facilitate Overseas Private Investment Corporation (OPIC) programs, OPIC has invested in a number of funds supporting sub-Saharan Africa development, including the Africa Catalyst

Fund (US$300 million focused on small- and medium-sized enterprise development), Africa Healthcare Fund (US$100 million focused on private healthcare delivery businesses, and ECP Africa Fund II, (US$523 million, focused on telecommunications, oil and gas, power, transportation, agribusiness, media, financial services and manufacturing.). Tailored products to support clean and renewable energy are a particular focus. Specific to South Africa, OPIC currently supports a US$70 million loan to Blue Financial Services Limited to expand lending to South African SMEs. The project will have a significant developmental impact on South Africa's unbanked SME sector by providing approximately 700 loans to urban and rural borrowers, over half of which are expected to be women. As such, the project will provide increased access to capital for many previously disadvantaged entrepreneurs. OPIC will open an office in Johannesburg in 2013 to support investment to key African countries through its financing and risk mitigation instruments. Additional information on OPIC programs that involve South Africa may be found on OPIC's website: http://www.opic.gov/investment-funds/africa.

Labor

Over the last 18 years, the South African government has replaced apartheid-era labor legislation with policies that emphasize employment security, fair wages, and decent working conditions. Under the aegis of the National Economic Development and Labor Council (NEDLAC), government, business and organized labor negotiate all labor laws, with the exception of laws pertaining to occupational health and safety. The law allows workers to form or join trade unions without previous authorization or excessive requirements. Labor unions that meet a locally negotiated minimum threshold of representation (often fifty percent plus one union member) are entitled to represent the entire workplace in negotiations with management. As the majority union or representative union, they may also extract agency fees from non-union members and any minority unions also present in the workplace. In some workplaces, this financial incentive has encouraged inter-union rivalries, including intimidation, as unions compete for the maximum share of employees in seeking the status of representative union. Trade union membership figures are imprecise but total membership as of 2011 was estimated at 3.5 million people, 26.1 percent of employment in the formal sector. This was a decrease of almost 5 percent from 2010.

The right to strike is protected under South African law. There were 2.8 million working days lost in 2011 as compared to 20.6 million working days lost in 2010. This represents a decline of 636 percent. About 208 working days were lost to work stoppages per 1,000 working South Africans in 2011, compared to 1,593 in 2010. The community, social and personal services industry endured 52.1 percent of all days lost, the most of any sector. In 2011, electricity, gas and water supply and the construction industries experienced relative industrial peace, recording two work stoppages each. Three employers locked out strikers during work stoppages in 2010 and 2011. There were few industrial disputes in 2011 involving municipal workers. In 2011, employees lost approximately R1.073 billion in wages due to participation in work stoppages, compared to R407 million in 2010. Data from the Department of Labor indicates more than 52.3 percent of strikes involving the mining and manufacturing sectors in 2011 lasted between 6 to 10 days, up 44.4 percent from the previous year.

For the first time in the post-apartheid era, almost all of the major 2012 strikes were wildcat strikes—strikes without the backing of trade unions—which left considerable uncertainty about the future of labor relations in the South African mining sector. Labor action started in the platinum sector in February, when workers at the Impala Platinum mine demanded a salary increment outside the collective bargaining process. Likewise, workers demanding a salary increment at the Lonmin Platinum mine in Marikana began a strike in August without regard to the collective agreement signed between unions and the company. Most of these strikes were extremely violent, with 45 killed and many others injured in Marikana, as well as much property damage. During this period, illegal strikes spread to other sectors such as gold and coal. Workers in the transport sector embarked on a legally protected two-week strike which turned violent, with at least two deaths and countless damage to property and injuries to bystanders and non-striking truck drivers. This strike led to some shortages of petroleum products, particularly in Gauteng Province. Farm workers, for the first time in the history of South African labor relations, also took to the streets in protest against low salaries. They demanded increases to the government-set minimum wage of R69-R75 per day. Protests by farm workers continued through the end of 2012. The South African Department of Labor was expected to review the minimum wage for farm workers in March 2013.

South African business argues that the labor market is rigid and over-regulation has constrained job creation and employment. Under pressure to preserve jobs in the face of Chinese competition, the Southern African

Clothing and Textile Workers' Union (SACTWU) in October 2011 agreed to a novel deal that allowed for lower salaries for new hires.

The government proposed amendments to each of the four main labor laws in 2010. Business groups and analysts claimed the proposals would make South Africa's labor regime more rigid and discourage job creation. Representatives of business, labor and government changed some of the more controversial amendments in extensive consultations at the National Economic Development and Labor Council (NEDLAC), and Parliament is expected to approve the four amendment bills in February 2013, after which President Zuma will sign them into law.

Major labor legislation includes:

The Labor Relations Act, in effect since 1995, provides fair dismissal guidelines, dispute resolution mechanisms, and retrenchment guidelines stating employers must consider alternatives to retrenchment and must consult all relevant parties when considering possible layoffs. The Act enshrines the right of workers to strike and of management to lock out striking workers. The Act created the Commission on Conciliation, Mediation, and Arbitration (CCMA) which can conciliate, mediate, and arbitrate in cases of labor dispute, and is required to certify an impasse in bargaining council negotiation before a strike can be called legally. The CCMA's caseload currently exceeds what was anticipated. Revisions seek to close a loophole in current legislation regarding the definition of employers and employees in the South African legal system. Amendments to the LRA deal with the regulation of labor brokers set the threshold for recognition of unions, strike ballots and protect temporary or contract workers.

The Basic Conditions of Employment Act, implemented in 1997, establishes a 45-hour workweek and minimum standards for overtime pay, annual leave, sick leave and notice of termination. The Act also outlaws child labor.

Further, it states that no employer may require or permit overtime except by agreement, and overtime may not be more than ten hours per week.

The Employment Equity Act of 1998 prohibits employment discrimination and requires large- and medium-sized companies to prepare affirmative action plans to ensure that black South Africans, women, and disabled persons are adequately represented in the workforce. The Employment Equity Act amendments would increase fines for non-compliance with employment equity measures and have a new provision of equal pay for work of equal value.

The Occupational Health and Safety Act, last amended in 1993, provides for occupational health and safety standards and gives the Department of Labor the right to inspect the workplace. The Mine, Health and Safety Act authorizes the Inspector of Mines to provide regulatory oversight for the mining industry.

The Skills Development Act of 1998 imposes an annual levy on employers equal to one percent of the payroll that is to be used for training programs devised by industry-specific training authorities (SETAs). Many groups, including organized business, question the effectiveness of SETAs. This concern has been magnified due to recent proposals to double the annual levy.

The most recent Quarterly Labor Force Survey (LFS) published in July 2012 listed the official unemployment rate at 24.5 percent. The LFS defines unemployment to exclude persons who have not actively sought employment during the previous four weeks.

The unemployment rate increases to 37.4 percent if these 2.2 million discouraged job seekers are included. Many unemployed people have never worked. Despite the high unemployment rate, South Africa has a shortage of skilled workers across many sectors.

South Africa has no country-wide minimum wage, but the Minister of Labor has issued determinations that set a minimum wage for certain occupations where collective bargaining is not common. These occupations include domestic workers, farm workers, and taxi drivers. More information regarding South African labor legislation can be found at: www.labour.gov.za/legislation.

Foreign Trade Zones/Free Ports

South Africa designated its first Industrial Development Zone (IDZ) in 2001. IDZs offer duty-free import of production-related materials and zero VAT on materials sourced from South Africa, along with the right to sell in South Africa upon payment of normal import duties on finished goods. Expedited services and other logistical arrangements may be provided for small to medium-sized enterprises, or for new foreign direct investment. Co-funding for infrastructure development is available from DTI. There are no exemptions from other laws or regulations, such as environmental and labor laws. The Manufacturing Development Board licenses IDZ enterprises in collaboration with the South African Revenue Service (SARS), which handles

IDZ customs matters. IDZ operators may be public, private, or a combination of both. IDZs are currently located at Coega near Port Elizabeth, in East London and Richards Bay.

There were plans for an IDZ at OR Tambo International Airport near Johannesburg, which have not been realized. In August 2012, the parliament passed a bill establishing the framework for creation of Special Economic Zones (SEZs).

The SEZs were intended to encompass the IDZs but also provide scope for economic activity beyond export-driven industry to include innovation centers and regional development. The DTI plans SEZs for Cape Town, Gauteng, Durban-Pietermaritzburg, East London and Port Elizabeth.

Foreign Direct Investment Statistics

Foreign direct investment (FDI) data is available in South Africa. The U.S. Embassy relies on the U.S. Department of Commerce and SARB for foreign investment data. SARB statistics conform to the IMF definition of FDI (i.e., ownership of at least 10 percent of the voting rights in an organization by a foreign resident or several affiliated foreign residents, including equity capital, reinvested earnings, and long-term loan capital) and represent actual investment to exclude announced but not completed "intended" investment. The SARB does not provide country-specific figures that distinguish between investment flows and changes in investment stocks from asset swaps, exchange rate adjustments, or mergers and acquisitions.

SARB statistics can be found at: www.reservebank.co.za – Publications – Quarterly Reports.

U.S. Companies with investment in South Africa of at least R10 million (US$1.4 million) include: Amazon, Amonix, Caltex, Caterpillar, Chevron, Coca-Cola, Corning, Cisco, CitiGroup, CSX, Dell, Dow Chemical, Eastman, Eli Lilly, First Solar, Ford, Forest Oil, Fluor, General Electric, General Motors, Goodyear, Honeywell, HP, IBM, Johnson & Johnson, Joy Global, Kimberly-Clark, Levi Strauss, McDonald's, Microsoft, Nike, Pioneer Energy, Proctor & Gamble, Sara Lee, Silicon Graphics, Solar Reserve, Timken, Walmart, Westinghouse, and Whirlpool.

The following FDI statistics were drawn from the SARB's September 2012 Quarterly Bulletin. The conversion exchange rate used was the average exchange rate for each year cited.

There was no update for 2011 figures.

Table A. Average Exchange Rates

Year	2005	2006	2007	2008	2009	2010
Rand/USD	6.36	6.76	7.05	8.25	8.43	7.32

Table B. Year-end Stock of Foreign Direct Investment in South Africa

	2004	2005	2006	2007	2008	2009	2010
Rand (billion)	362.86	499.59	611.72	751.92	632.61	866.66	1015.52
USD (billion)	57.05	78.55	90.49	106.66	76.68	102.81	138.73

Table C. Year-end stock of FDI in South Africa by region/country

REGION/COUNTRY	2008	2009	2010	2008	2009	2010
CURRENCY(billion)	Rand	Rand	Rand	USD	USD	USD
EUROPE - Total	492.3	697.4	850.03	59.67	82.73	116.12
N/S America - Total	65.1	80.14	62.732	7.89	9.5	10.04
USA	47.1	55.83	73.47	5.7	6.62	8.57
AFRICA	5.2	5.9	6.5	.63	.70	.89
ASIA	68.1	81.4	83.88	8.25	9.66	11.46
OCEANIA	1.6	1.6	1.52	.19	.19	
TOTAL	679.4	922.27	1078.13	82.35	109.4	147.28

Table D. FDI Flows into South Africa (USD millions)

2005	2006	2007	2008	2009	2010
6.65094	-0.5325	5.68794	9.01818	5.39383	1.22814

INDEX

D

E

F

G

T